COUNTRY NOTES

COUNTRY NOTES

V. SACKVILLE-WEST

ITH PHOTOGRAPHS BY BRYAN AND NORMAN WESTWOOD

Essay Index Reprint Series

Essay Index

BOOKS FOR LIBRARIES PRESS
FREEPORT, NEW YORK

INTERNATIONAL STANDARD BOOK NUMBER:
0-8369-2072-4

LIBRARY OF CONGRESS CATALOG CARD NUMBER:
77-117835

PRINTED IN THE UNITED STATES OF AMERICA

ACKNOWLEDGMENTS

MOST of these notes have appeared at fortnightly intervals during 1938 and 1939 in the *New Statesman and Nation*, and I would wish to record my gratitude to the editor not only for his permission to reprint them, but also for his suggestion that I should write them. My thanks are also due to *Harper's Bazaar*, *Vogue*, *Time and Tide*, *Travel*, and the Committee for the Preservation of Rural Kent, for permission to reprint respectively ' Gardens and Gardeners ', ' Circus ', ' Tuscany ', ' French Savoy ', ' The Kentish Landscape '. ' The Garden and the Oast ' originally appeared in *The Nation and Athenæum*, and again I must thank the editor of the *New Statesman and Nation* for allowing me to make use of it.

Finally my warmest thanks are due to Mr. Bryan and Mr. Norman Westwood for their co-operation and their admirable photographs.

CONTENTS

PHOTOGRAPHS

By BRYAN & NORMAN WESTWOOD

A Country Life

LIVING in the country as I do, I sometimes stop short to ask myself where the deepest pleasure is to be obtained from a rural life, so readily derided as dull by the urban-minded. When I stop short like this, it is usually because some of my metropolitan friends have arrived to ruffle my rustic peace with the reverberations of a wider world. They ask me if I have seen this or that play, these or those pictures, and always I find myself obliged to reply that I have not. This makes me appear, and feel, a boor. Then after this most salutary visit they drive off, back to London, and the peace and the darkness close down on me once more, leaving me slightly disturbed but on the whole with an insulting sense of calm superiority. They leave me feeling that I am getting more out of this short life than they for all their agitations, an attitude of mind which strikes me as intolerably self-righteous. How can I possibly justify it ? Should I not believe that it is more important to concern oneself with the troubles and interests of the world, than to observe the first crocus in flower ? More important to take an active part wherever one's small activity would be most welcome, than to grow that crocus ? How, then, to explain my backwater's deep source of delight ?

I suppose the pleasure of country life lies really in the eternally renewed evidences of the determination to live. That is a truism when said, but anything but a truism when daily observed. Nothing shows up the difference between the thing said or read, so much as the daily experience of it. The small green shoot appearing one day at the base of a plant one had feared dead, brings a comfort and an encouragement for which the previous daily observance is responsible. The life principle has proved unconquerable, then, in spite of frost and winds ? The powers of resistance against adversity are greater than we thought ; the germ of life lies hidden even in the midst of apparent death. A cynic might contend that nothing depressed him more than this resoluteness to keep going ; it depends on the angle from which you regard this gallant tenacity. For my own part I find a singular solace in the renewal and reality of even the most monotonous of natural processes ; I welcome the youth of the new season, whether it comes with the first lambs to be born in a snow-storm or with the new buds of the hornbeam pushing the old brown leaves off the hedges. If you have a taste for such things, no amount of repetition can stale them ; they stand for permanence in a changing world.

January

RIMBAUD wrote a famous sonnet about the characteristics of the five vowels, A was black, E white, I red, and so on. This somewhat precious conception might be extended to the months of the year. January, to me, is a large pewter plate stained with the reflection of a red sunset ; and no doubt others will have their own ideas.

I do not like January very much. It is too stationary. Not enough happens. I like the evidences of life, and in January there are too few of them. It is true that you can find buds on the hazels, and that the small leaves of the wild honeysuckle are already formed and green, but that means very little since everybody knows that the honeysuckles, like the lilacs, seldom close down their business. It is also true that snowdrops and some of the narcissi are coming through the ground, but somehow this does not give me the same pleasure as it would in February. I do not like either plants or children to be precocious. As for the tulip leaves which this year have appeared long before they ought to have been seen at all, no gardener could view them with anything but concern.

On the other hand, the true beauties of January are welcome —the bare trees, the wild, wet sky, even the cart-ruts full of water, and the sea-gulls settling on the plough. It is very much the month for a country walk. The small streams are so angry, that even the most exiguous trickle has turned into a minute brown waterfall. Twigs swirl as they are rushed towards the sea. Broken branches lie in disarray, giving a careless air to our trim rides ; the wood-pigeons' old nests at the tops of the trees make dark untidy blobs as they nakedly sway. Damp and dishevelled, January is the month for thick shoes, a dog at our heels, and the wind in our faces.

Winter Colour

THE dog-wood has seemed more brilliant than ever this winter, perhaps owing to the fact that it has nearly always been wet. Dog-wood, like porphyry, gains in intensity from being wet, and to see the red dog-wood at its best you should sweep suddenly round a bend on a rainy evening with the headlights of your car streaming across it. Then the glistening stems, naked and red from base to tip, stand up like a phalanx of savages bathed in blood. Descriptions of plants usually sound so much better than the reality, but it is not possible to exaggerate the startling effect of *Cornus sanguinea* seen in the right light.

A little winter-flowering tree the oddity of which cannot be exaggerated either is the witch-hazel. The dark brown twigs look as though some child had amused itself by tying them up with bunches of yellow ribbons, and then snipping the ends short. The little bunches flutter all the way up the stems, each secured at the base by a maroon button. There are no leaves at all ; the twigs are quite bare save for the numerous yellow stars. Like the wintersweet, the witch-hazel has the faculty of growing in so delicate a design that one might believe them both to be possessed of a sense of drawing as fine as their countrymen the Chinese, in a spare precision that exactly suits the brown earth and grey skies. They have more than stylisation : they have style.

Such economy makes the Christmas roses look tousled and undistinguished as they cower beneath the umbrella of their leaves, but strip all leaves away, and then, in a clear glass, the separate flowers stand out in purity, ice-green and white like blown anemones. It is a very definite improvement on nature, to deprive some flowers of their leaves. The common white syringa, which one ought to call philadelphus, becomes quite a different thing under such treatment ; great branches of it in a tall vase

15

look unrecognisably like some rare white almond ; and the wild crab-apple of the hedgerows, its shell-pink blossom clinging against the bough hoary with grey lichen, achieves a delicacy that the furnished bough never possessed. But best of all are the winter flowerers which have discovered this secret of elegance for themselves without submitting to such vandalism.

February Frost

Some mornings and evenings lately have enjoyed an extraordinary beauty. The early frosts have glittered as white as a fresh snowfall, bushes and hedges have been looped with silver threads, and the rime on the tall trees has turned them into frozen fountains. There has been a motionless quality about

17

these mornings, through which the bird-song has chinked as clearly as breaking glass.   Under a pale blue sky the white pigeons wheel like a squadron in formation, white no longer, but blue in the shadows and gold where the sun catches their wings.   The Chinese fix little devices on to their pigeons, which in flight give off a faint music like a multitude of tiny Æolian harps.   Even without this pretty artifice, there can be few sounds lovelier than the silken swoop of wings as they settle, and their contented cooing almost persuades one to believe that the day is warm.   Their pink feet make the frozen grass blades bend ; bowing and prinking, they peck delicately for grains, then at an unseen signal they are in flight again, to settle this time in a colony on the tiled roof of a barn.

There is still a film of ice over shady stretches of water, so thin that by midday the breasts of the ducks cut with a brittle tinkling sound through it like miniature ice-breakers in formation. By the evening it has closed up again, and now reflects the large lemon-coloured moon in a trance of breathless stillness. Mist rises from the valley, a cold white mist, cutting off everything but the tops of the trees. A solitary swan sails in plumed ghostliness, round and round in the only patch of water left open to him. All else is quiet, shrouded for the long hours of the night which are to follow.

Spring in Illyria

THE talented author of *Peking Picnic* once wrote a novel called *Illyrian Spring*. I thought it not one of her most successful works, if she will forgive me for saying so, but it remained settled in my mind for her descriptions of the flowers which leap from the rocks of the country we now call Dalmatia. I remember those passages at least once a year when my heart is torn between the desire to go south and the desire to remain in England. This moment occurs at any time between March the first and the end of April, and it coincides with the recollection that the Mediterranean flora must be beginning to put on its best. On a dead grey day, when nothing seems to be stirring and a small sour wind is mourning across the fields, I find myself seized with a desire to steal the motor car out of the garage, drive myself to Dover, and embark on the first vessel which will put me within reach of the sunny flowery shores. All this, without saying a word to anyone. Just to disappear. To disappear suddenly, without any explanation. To go away ; to vanish ; to abandon all one's responsibilities and commitments ; to live for a month given up to the pure pursuit of visual beauty. How great that beauty can be, how lavish that floral explosion, no one needs to be reminded who remembers the ruins of Greece pouring with wild flowers, the slopes of the Lebanon, the craggy coasts of Illyria.

The truth is that we all make the mistake here of expecting spring to arrive earlier than it means to. The first buds and blossoms cause our hearts to run ahead in an anticipation which will not be fulfilled for at least a month later than we begin to expect it. Spring, in England, in a normal year (if such a thing exists) does not ostensibly show itself until the second fortnight of April. These occasional, deliciously tender days are the fairest of the year's delusions, though from year to year it is impossible to

20

remain wisely sceptical. The first mild sunshine, the first morning with the missel-thrush singing on the topmost branch, and we are instantly persuaded that these things have come to stay. Thus although from December 1st to March 1st I can cheerfully endure the discipline of the English winter, comforting myself with the old belief that such harshness is good for the soul and compensated by the naked beauty it brings to those who have the eye to see, yet by March 1st I grow impatient. Surely spring should not delay so long, when one has only to go elsewhere to find it ?

The Flowery Shelf

YET there are special considerations which reconcile me to the necessity for staying at home, and which indeed would make me reluctant in some ways to take my departure. These considerations are focused on a long narrow shelf in a cold greenhouse, where pans of diminutive Alpines are coming into flower. Here, at least, is a place where I can pretend that the year is a month older than it actually is. Very soon this shelf will be a solid pavement of colour. Already the earlier saxifrages are in flower ; bright pinks and yellows much larger and more exuberant than the squabs of grey tufts which they so successfully dwarf. The whole point, I think, of the Alpines, as of certain people, is that in the rare moment of their blooming they transcend their tight habitual personality. They have something of the quality of the habitually silent reserved person who suddenly and without any warning exposes himself or herself in a single phrase of self-revelation, brief but beautiful. One knows it will not endure, but one has seen the light.

The light that the little Alpines expose is rare and exquisite and delicate. For that reason alone I maintain that they ought to be grown under glass. No one could possibly dislike forced flowers more than I do, but Alpines grown under glass in a cold house cannot be said to be artificially forced into flower before their time. One is merely protecting them from the smashes of rain and the splashes of mud which would destroy their particular beauty. The sensitiveness of *Primula Winteri*, for instance, battered by winds and rains, the mealy powdering of its leaves, the tenderness of its lavender petals—where would all these things be, delivered harshly to our winter weather ?

The nicety, the extreme fragility, of these small things recalls the art of that great craftsman—great in a small way—the Russian

Fabergé.   He made jewelled flowers of jade, coral, quartz, and pearls to adorn Edwardian drawing-rooms.   An artist, he worked his small conceits in a manner suited only to the offensively rich people able to buy them.   I am told that Fabergé plants command a high price in the market to-day.   I would not exchange one of them against one of the real little pans I have flowering cheaply in my cold Alpine house.

Out in the open, too, life is stirring.   There are two black-birds so intent upon making a nest that I scarcely worry them when I pass.   The ring-doves cut past me on wings sharp as blades.   They go scything through the air in a manner to slice off the almond blossom.   So gentle and yet so sharp.   Then they settle and coo, amorous as the spring, tender as a girl newly in love.

Country Speech

How much one regrets that local turns of speech should be passing away! There was a freshness and realism about them which kept the language alive and can never be replaced. Imported into prose they become fossilised and affected, for, accurately reported though they may be in those novels of rural life of which one grows so tired, the spontaneity and even the accent are lacking; imported into poetry, they instantly sound like the archaisms of a poetic convention. If I read the phrase, ' The cattle do be biding in the meads ', it gives me no pleasure at all, but if a cowman says it to me (as he once actually did) it fills me with delight. I like also being informed that the rabbits are ' interrupting ' or ' interfering with ' the young trees ; at least, I do not like the fact, but the way in which it is conveyed does much to mitigate my annoyance. I resent the mud less when I am told that the cows have ' properly slubbed it up '. Then sometimes comes a proverbial ring : ' He talks too much, talk and do never did lie down together.' I do not see where we are to find such refreshing imagery in future, unless, indeed, we look to America where the genius of the vivid phrase still seems to abide.

The Knitter

I HAVE a friend who knits. She sits on the floor, the firelight glancing on her hair, her tartan scarf thrown over her shoulders. She and the wide brick fireplace and the clicking needles and the balls of wool heaped on the floor beside her, would compose a complete Dutch-school picture, were it not for the tartan scarf which suggests a crofter's cottage. She, oblivious of such objective considerations, continues to knit. She does not care whether she looks Dutch or Scottish ; whether she fits into the tiled interior rosy as a pippin, or into the shieling. Nor do I care either. All that I know is that whenever she condescends to visit me, she, with her scarf and her wools, adds colour to the warm evening hour, when it has grown too dark to·go out and one sits over the fire and talks.

Talks. . . . There is the snag. One cannot, I find, talk to a knitter. Conversation may seem to be going in that greased, easy way essential to all good conversation ; starting hares too lavishly to follow them up ; allowing pauses for rumination ; bursts for sudden eagerness ; digressions, returns, new departures, discoveries of rooted creeds or new ideas—sooner or later the challenge is bound to come : " Don't you agree ? " or " What do you think ? " " Yes ? " says the knitter, startled but polite, " seventy-five, seventy-six—just a moment till I get to the end of my row—seventy-seven, seventy-eight—yes," she says, looking up brightly, " it's all right now. What were you saying ? " But of course one has forgotten or no longer cares.

All the same, everyone who wants to add a coloured domestic touch to that pleasant idle hour which comes between tea and dinner should engage a permanent knitter, dumb if necessary but ornamental. There is something soothing to the nerves about the monotony of the long needles travelling up and down the line ; something satisfying to the eye about this primitive craft so closely allied to netting and weaving. A lace-maker rattling the bobbins on her pillow would make too much noise, and the whiteness of her work would jar too crudely on the hush and dimness of the room. The knitter with her wools, curled up beside the fire, is precisely what is needed. So long as you do not expect her to talk.

Jacob's Sheep

MY occasional annoyance with this particular knitter is tempered by the fact that she uses the wool spun from the fleeces of my own sheep. This gives me a self-supporting feeling, especially as I live in the district which was once the centre of the cloth industry in England. Moreover, my sheep are peculiar sheep ; splotched and horned, people usually take them for goats at first sight. They have a most romantic ancestry, for not only are they supposed to be descended from those flocks—ringstraked, speckled, and spotted—which Jacob increased by such remarkable pre-natal methods in the land of Laban, but other picturesque legends also enter into their history. In actual fact, nobody seems to know anything about them at all, and a high authority whom I consulted suggests that they now appear to be in existence only in this country, rather a sad fate for animals whose origin has been variously attributed to Syria, Portugal, North Africa, Zululand, Persia, Egypt, and Barbary. It is also related that the Crusaders brought them from the Holy Land ; and that they arrived in England via Spain, either wrecked on the coast of Ireland with a ship of the Armada, or were, less dramatically, presented to George III by a lady named the Marquesa del Campo de Alange. This version, however, undoubtedly refers to the breed of Spanish merinos and not to Jacob's sheep at all. Merinos do not thrive in our climate, even under Royal patronage ; Edward IV, who imported three thousand from Spain, had already failed to make a success of them. Jacob's sheep, on the other hand, thrive and multiply ; the ewes habitually give birth to twins and even triplets ; their enormous fleeces safeguard them from cold and damp ; they are said to be hardier than our native breeds. The old gentleman who has charge of my small flock here has a pleasing theory about them : he is persuaded that they come

from a mountainous country and that they stand for preference on the emmet-heaps as the nearest thing they can find to a mountain in Kent. As he is old enough to remember ploughing the fields here with a yoke of oxen, he ought to know.

In May or June, after shearing, we send the sacks of wool to the Highlands to be cleaned and spun. A bundle of sample colours comes back, which I have learned to call a swatch. Skeins (which I have learned to call cuts) are the next thing to arrive, dyed to our requirements. Wound into balls, they are heaped into great baskets till the knitter wants them, a warm harvest of gaudy fruits. Since our correspondents in the north treat their affairs in a leisurely way, suggesting that the spirit of bustle has not yet infected Inverness, the autumn is usually well advanced before this luxuriance can be piled in a corner of the room. The orange balls on the floor echo the Jaffa oranges on the table ; the green ones repeat the bowl of gourds ; the purple the last belated figs ; the red the first apples. Since Jacob's sheep in Jacob's day were so suggestible as to produce skewbald lambs after Jacob had shown them his peeled poplar wands, what would be the effect, I wonder, if I were to show my ewes this basket of their own wool, on the lambs which I shall expect next March ?

The Heron

EVERY morning at dawn the heron comes winging across the woods to rob my lake of its trout. It is not a very large lake, and there are not very many trout ; soon there will be none at all if the heron continues to breakfast in this fashion. I would not grudge him a reasonable meal occasionally, but he is an indiscriminate and extravagant fisherman who pulls out trout too large for him to swallow and strews them mangled on the bank. The good fisherman, the honest angler, returns his smaller catch to the water ; the heron acts contrariwise, failing to return those which are too big to be of any use to him. The other day he was seen struggling with one half way down his throat ; and in spite of my liking for herons, especially when they frequent other people's lakes and streams, I confess I wish it had choked him.

The remedy may seem simple : shoot the heron. But there is a snag : the heron is a protected bird, with the price of five pounds on his head. I discovered this only when I had finally overcome my reluctance to destroy so beautiful a creature and was about to construct a murderous ' hide ' in the wood near his haunt. The country people were quite at a loss to understand my hesitation, and their advice was unanimous : shoot him and say

nothing about it. When I said I couldn't square that with my conscience they looked at me pityingly.

Meanwhile he continues to breakfast and the trout to diminish. Although we have tried ' warming his tail ' without injuring him he does not seem to mind having his tail warmed. So what am I to do ? I could, of course, walk up to the local police station with a dead bird in one hand and a five-pound note in the other. But although that would set me right in my own eyes and in those of the law, it still would not dispose of my conviction that if the law troubles to protect the heron it means that he needs protection, and that without it he will soon disappear from our ponds and water courses. Which I, for one, would regret.

30

The Lake

THE lake did not exist when first I came to the place, but an
obviously artificial embankment surrounding two marshy
meadows suggested that water had once filled the hollow. Judging
by the age of the oaks that grew on the embankment, it must have
been created two or three centuries ago. A little stream ran down
from the wood, and to dam the stream was two days' work. Three
days later a sheet of water lay placidly where the useless swamp
had been, a most dramatic transformation, so simply, cheaply,
and easily achieved.

Since that day the lake has been a delight, revealing a whole
region of wild life I had never known before : water-birds, water-
insects, water-plants, and the general peacefulness of water life.
There are few things to compare with the tranquillity of even a
small piece of water at any hour out of the twenty-four, whether
at dawn, midday, sunset, or midnight ; spring, summer, autumn,
or winter ; few things so well adapted to repair the cracked heart,
the jangled temper, or the uneasy soul. The very reflection of
trees in water suggests how true and untrue life may be : the
solid oak as we see it growing on the bank, the mirrored reflection
—truth in untruth, the one no more convincing than the other.
There, surprisingly, lay the new lake, symbol of many things I
had always desired ; a piece of water, calm, rich, profound,
agitated, peaceful ; a mirror of life both false and true. It was a
creation romantic beyond my hopes. Extravagantly I ordered a
boat from the Army and Navy Stores.

The pleasure that one takes in a piece of water is also, in large
part, mixed with childish pleasure. It is all very well to say that
one meditates on the illusions of life as a grown-up : one also
paddles one's toes and trails one's fingers in that queerly different
element, water ; watches the tadpoles' wriggling capsules of soot ;

observes the gradual spread of bulrushes and thinks of Moses on one's nannie's lap ; watches the dragon-flies among the reeds, darting off on their blue and brown nuptial flight, so macilent, so oddly joined and jointed, so busy with something that as a child one only partly understood. One had read Madam How and Lady Why, but both Madam and Lady had been reluctant to

give the full explanation of those indicated mysteries.   One
simply observed the insects at their unexplained busyness and
wondered what they were at, and wished also that dragon-flies
two-and-a-half-feet across might still exist, and regretted that
such dragons were only to be found fossilised in such dull dead
things as carboniferous deposits.   A dragon-fly with a two-and-a-
half-foot wing span would indeed be an insect worth looking at ;
an alarming insect, an aeroplane in miniature.   Instead of these,
we are left with the common dragon-flies : flies of our ponds and
lakes, beautiful enough but sizeably unworthy of St. George and
his lance.   Since we cannot have humming-birds in this country,
we have to make shift with dragon-flies and kingfishers.   The
dragon-fly and the kingfisher are the humming-birds of England.
Kingfishers do not frequent my lake as frequently as I should
like ; only twice have I seen that surprising flash of blue.   Never
have I found the dirty nest dug into the bank.   Yet I continue
to look and to hope, and meanwhile the tadpoles and dragon-flies
satisfy me, since the pleasure one derives from a piece of water
is a very simple, unexorbitant pleasure.

Trout

THE trout came as a surprise, overbrimming the cup of pleasure. True, the first indication of their presence came in a depressing fashion, for they got drowned and my first sight of them was of a row of ten fat speckled corpses, neatly laid out for my inspection. Until then I should have imagined that drowning was the last death a fish was ever likely to encounter, but there they were, lying *bel et bien* drowned by muddy water in a shallow pocket of the lake which we had been obliged to empty for the purpose of repairing a leak in the bank. The poor things had evidently followed the flowing water during the night to the last place where water still collected, and the mud had been too much for them and the water too little. Beautiful well-fed trout they were too, turning the scales between a pound and a half to two pounds ; many flies and many water-snails must have gone to their keeping.

This was the opinion of an expert, who obligingly undertook to supply a consignment of fingerlings from his hatchery. I had never heard the expression before, and listened to his specialised wisdom in the mood of meekness which overcomes one in the presence of someone possessed of a technical vocabulary which appears to be English but bears little relation to the language one commonly employs. One nods intelligently every now and then to indicate that one has understood, but if one were honest one would interrupt constantly by saying that one really hadn't grasped the meaning at all. This is the kind of discourse which forces one into the dishonesty of sorting out, bit by bit, what the all-too-well-advised man is talking about. In this furtive way I learnt that fingerlings meant very young trout, the length of a finger ; I learnt also a lot of things about caddis-worms and snails and bottom-feed, which had never entered into my philosophy. I came away from this conversation feeling enriched.

The fingerlings duly arrived by lorry, in containers like milk-churns, with elaborate instructions accompanying them. It is far less simple than one would think to tip two hundred young trout into a lake. One has to mix the water by degrees, accustoming them gradually to the element they will presently have to swim in. It takes a whole afternoon mixing the water of the churns with the water of the lake before one can tip the whole consignment into its final home. Yet it is satisfactory, in the end, to pour a milk-churn full of young fish into the larger waters, knowing that they will wriggle away happily into the liberty of the placid water, and find therein a number of snails they can devour.

The fingerlings have grown. The expert who said that the bottom-feed was good has been justified in his opinion : the trout that we now pull out are fine fish, turning three and a half pounds on the scale. My feelings when these big trout are caught are mixed : I feel proud of such big trout being caught in the lake I so easily created, and have no desire to address them in the somewhat surprising words of Leigh Hunt :

> O scaly, slippery, wet, swift, staring wights,
> What is't ye do ? What life lead ? Eh, dull goggles ?
> How do ye vary your vile days and nights ?
> How pass your Sundays ?

Then I feel sorry for the innocent fingerlings I introduced to a happy home ; then I feel pleased for the fisherman who has had the satisfaction of hooking and playing a dashing fish.

The person I do resent, and also admire, is the heron who discovered the trout weeks before anyone else knew they were there and who has pursued his discovery ever since.

Early Hours

I WONDER whether the freshness of these early spring mornings really intoxicates the birds as much as we believe ? Judging by their song as the sun rises, it is easy to credit them with feelings of exhilaration similar to our own. Even those who do not express themselves in song must surely.catch the infection from this young, budding, courting air. My heron, for instance, as he flaps his way from his home-pond to my suffering lake, can surely not remain indifferent to the brightening sky and the clean chill meeting his wings above the frosty fields ? ~~The spring world, seen from above at dawn, empty of men,~~ must glitter with an ~~extraordinary purity, miraculously~~ combining both the virginal ~~and the pregnant.~~ To rise even an hour earlier than usual, is to steal a march upon the midge-like bothers of the common day ; it is to live; however briefly, in the illusion of a different world.

Statistics prove that the beginning of March is normally colder than the beginning of December, though this year statistics have proved, as usual, unreliable. Only he who has gone out into the fields early knows that the grass has been white and spangled, and that there has been a sharp nip in the air. On these still, cloudless mornings, under a pale blue sky, the first delicate flowers have stood out with a peculiar brilliance, almost as though they were being illuminated with artificial light. It is remarkable how many of the flowers that appear in a notoriously boisterous season are more delicate and fragile than their successors : the petals of the crocus and of the early irises look as though they could scarcely survive a puff of wind ; the slender stems of the blue squills and glory-of-the-snow look as though they would snap and bend at a touch. The starry blue anemone, the minute narcissus, the inch-high saxifrages, all seeming to demand the protection of glass, do nothing of the sort but choose the roughest

of months to lift their childish heads in the open. The blossom, too, though this year the bright days have suited it well, is more often to be seen through the veils of a scurrying snowstorm. This year the pink of the naked almond stands out against the blue, and the white of plum dazzles in the sun. Young plum-trees are a sight to stand and gaze at, the blossom so white, the branches so black. They compromise no more than a woodcut in their colour, or absence of colour.

To see these sights, unshared, unspoiled, is worth the lost hour in bed.

The Urchin Wakes

THE moment is near at hand when one no longer wishes merely to ' stand and stare ', but also to look about for things not obviously revealed. Not only are the birds thinking about their nests, but the hibernating animals are beginning to emerge. The squirrels (which, indeed, are not true hibernators) have been active for some weeks past, and the evening is not far distant when a dog will grow frantic as he discovers a hedgehog shuffling along under a hedge. You can collect the hedgehog if you like, and make a pet of him with bribes of bread-and-milk, but if you have no taste or time for such school-boyish occupations there is still some amusement to be derived from the study of any stray earth-pig you may meet in the course of a walk. For one thing you may consider respectfully that in this queer prickly object, probably very untidy at this time of year, since leaves and bits of moss from his winter home still remain impaled upon his prickles, like some grotesque Ophelia, you have the representative of one of the oldest inhabitants of Britain. The earth-pig was here before man was ; he is extremely ancient, and truly indigenous. In fact, he has probably not changed his appearance at all since long before a caricature of man first shambled round on Piltdown. This alone confers on him a dignity which is not shared even by the badger, our little British bear, and certainly not by the rabbit, that upstart foreigner who claims, with more justification than most of our aristocracy, to have arrived on these shores with William the Conqueror. But there are other reasons which may endear the hedgehog to his compatriots. Watch him as he hunts for food, so busy and thorough : he wins the admiration of all who dislike slipshod methods. Or pick him up (remembering, however, that he is covered with fleas) and put him at the angle of two walls, so that he has no escape except by going over. Stoutly he sets himself to climb.   It is a dogged rather than a nimble performance. For every few inches gained, he makes a mistake and falls to the ground, rolling himself quickly into a ball as he tumbles, so that he may bounce on his prickles and take no harm.   When he does eventually reach the top, he rolls himself off down the other side, though I suspect that this is due to accident rather than to design.

Hedgehogs eat snakes among other things ; and although the bite of even an adder cannot harm him the wily pig does not see the fun of allowing himself to be bitten when he can dispatch his victim by the means nature has provided.   So he merely gives a preliminary nip to provoke the snake (for unless he can bite just below the head he cannot hope to kill outright) and then rapidly rolls himself into a ball before the fangs can strike him.   Hurt and enraged, the snake attacks, too angry to notice his own wounds, until the moment comes for the hedgehog to unroll and start a leisurely meal, from the tail upwards.   I have never had the good fortune to see such a combat, but I live in hopes.

Eternities of Kitchen Garden

THE conservatism of our island race seems to begin with our vegetables. Rows and rows of cabbages, rows and rows of sprouts. . . . The sameness of kitchen gardens appals the thoughtful epicure looking out of railway carriage windows. However ill-informed a gardener, his eye never lights upon a plant he cannot instantly identify. He may well ask if enterprise is totally lacking, the sense of adventure entirely dead, among these cultivators of the homely plot? The answer is: They are.

Yet there is no reason why the amateur epicure should go unsatisfied. Variety can be his for a few pence and a little extra trouble ; not many pence and not much trouble. He grows cabbages already, does he, in his own kitchen garden patch? Then why not grow the red cabbage as well as the green? There exists a theory in this country that red cabbage is meant for pickling and for pickling only, a theory demonstrably fallacious. He grows potatoes : then why not vary the floury English kinds with some handfuls of the French, which may be obtained under such charming names as Belle de Juillet, and which are of a far better and firmer consistency? He grows tomatoes, no doubt, but has he tried the fruit tomato, something like a myrobolan plum to look at, red or yellow? Has he tried cooking the young shoots of the common hop, or of the poke-weed, both of which resemble asparagus? Has he tried eating his vegetable marrows when they are four or five inches long, instead of letting them grow into watery giants fit for nothing but the local flower-show? (The more he picks, the more they will crop.) Has he given up an odd corner to growing sorrel, that weed demanding no care, which may be picked as early as February and used either like spinach or as a soup? (*soupe à l'oseille*). Has he any globe artichokes, as handsome in grey-green leaf as they are useful as a vegetable?

41

All these are simple, but a step forward in ambition and the possession of a warm greenhouse will give him Indian corn on the cob, also the succulent egg-plant (aubergine) and even pimento if he cares for it.

This list is a short one and is really designed only to send the kitchen gardener back to the catalogues where he will find further suggestions and also instructions. Our nurserymen, some of them, seem to be getting more enterprising, even if their customers have not yet followed their example. The most engaging suggestion which I have come across, however, hails from France. It is called ' Innocent surprises for the salad ', and by means of a few packets of seed enables you to grow fruits charmingly deceptive as caterpillars, snails, worms, and hedgehogs.

Better though not Bigger Fruit

WRITING about vegetables reminds me of several grievances I hold against fruit-growers also. In many of her counties England is very definitely a fruit-growing country ; witness the clouds of blossom which float over miles of orchard during April and May. Late frosts, hailstorms, and lack of sun are of course the unconquerable enemies, but although we may never hope to rival the jewelled, Mantegna-like swags and garlands of southerly climates—those lemons, those oranges, those grapes, those apricots, all so rich, heavy, and glowing—we still contrive to make a fair show both with our blossom in the spring and our country-cheeked apples and cherries in the late summer. There are moments when I feel I would not exchange all the groves of grape-fruit and peaches in California for the sight of an English orchard, its boughs weighted down with fruit and all the pleasant cheerful business of picking going on.

But to return to my grievance. I do wonder why the amateur fruit-grower in this on the whole favoured country should content himself with the meagre variety he allows his garden to provide. Gooseberries—yes, they are very well, and their hairy paunches explode agreeably against the palate when pressed by the tongue. Raspberries—they are very well too, especially, as somebody remarked, for the first hundred times. Currants, too, red, black, and white, are very good, particularly when damped in their bunches and then dipped in castor sugar. But the amateur's garden will do much better for him than that, if he gives it the chance. Has he grown the pink currant ? Probably not. Has he discovered the Alpine strawberry, for which he will ungrudgingly pay an exorbitant price when it appears on the menu as *Fraises des bois* on his continental holiday ? If he hasn't, let me tell him that in the Alpine strawberry (which is quite as easy to grow as any other strawberry) he will find a fruit in every way superior to the rather woody little berry provided as *Fraises des bois*—larger, less ' seedy ', more luscious altogether, and with the advantage of a longer fruiting season than the ordinary strawberry, lasting, in fact, well into the autumn. Has he tried figs against a south wall ? It is a mistake to think that outdoor figs will ripen only in southern Europe ; they will ripen perfectly in the southern counties in an average English summer. Given the protection of glass (unheated) they will even provide two crops during the year. Peaches and nectarines, also, are too rarely planted, yet they fruit exuberantly against a wall exposed to the sun. Any house, however small, can supply such a wall ; its owner would be better advised to plant a peach or a nectarine against it than the tangle of Dorothy Perkins or American Pillar under which such walls are usually disguised.

The Vineyards of England

ENGLAND had her vineyards once, so there seems to be no reason why she should not have them again. They enjoy the prestige of mention in Domesday Book, and they grew on the south slopes of the North Downs. They have long since receded into history, and the descendants of our original vintagers have quite given up the idea of growing the grape vine now for their own benefit. Here and there a solitary vine exists to provide its bunches annually, which in due course are turned into an excruciatingly nasty drink labelled ' Home-made wine ' by cottage-wives, equivalent to other home-made wines such as ' cowslip ' and ' elder-berry ', whose names carry a charmingly old-world suggestion so long as the decoction remains in the bottle, but not once it has left the bottle for the glass.

In spite of this scepticism taught by experience, I see no reason why grape-vines should not still be grown more freely out-of-doors in the south of England. Even if we refrain from making our own wine, there is a certain satisfaction in heaping a plate with some dark bunches, however tasteless, however watery, of our own growing. The names alone of hardy vines provide an ornament to the garden ; they remind one vaguely of the troubadours and the Crusades : Primavere Frontignan, Muscatel, Muscadine, Black Prince. The leaves in themselves are very beautiful, both in design and colour—bright green in the spring, dark red in the autumn ; what more could be asked of any leaf ? I used to dry the most brilliant and perfectly shaped ones between blotting-paper pressed under two volumes of the *Encyclopædia Britannica*, after which they used to lie about in the unhappy way of things which have neither use nor a place of their own, until such time as an impatient schoolroom maid, saying she couldn't put up with my dust-traps any longer, would throw them all into the fire.

47

Scrape

IN conversation with a farmer friend, I recently learnt of the existence of this complaint—not to be confused with scrapie, which, as all readers are no doubt well aware, is due to a small parasite or sarcocyst lodging in the ovine muscular system. No. The complaint called scrape has a far more endearing origin than a mere parasitic insect producing excessive itchiness and consequent loss of wool. It is nothing less than homesickness ; it occurs only in sheep pining for their native land.

The native land, in this case, happens to be the Highlands of Scotland. You cannot, it appears, buy Highland sheep and bring them to the south of England without their becoming infected

with this most inconvenient disease.   The odd thing about it is that the first generation does not suffer ; it is only in the lambs that the homesickness begins to work.   They start by pawing the ground uneasily (hence the name *scrape*), they pine ; and if not speedily restored to their ancestral hills they die.   The only remedy, according to my friend, is to cross the breed with a southern ram, when the North apparently agrees to settle down comfortably with the South.   What an example for Queen Elizabeth.   If only she had known about scrape, she would certainly have arranged an English marriage for Mary Queen of Scots.

Flora
&
Fauna

ALL nature is explosive now with the frenzy of production. Every morning it becomes more necessary to discover what has happened during the night. Lambs appear, calves appear, nests are made, eggs are laid, leaves develop, flowers open. Already a vixen has removed a litter of cubs from their home in too close proximity to the house, carrying them one by one by the scruff as a cat will carry kittens or a squirrel her young, trotting seriously with them to a safer spot. Few babies, I suppose, enjoy a more unsettled nursery than some fox-cubs, and the habit of constant *déménagement* must become part of their psychological make-up at a very early age. The smell of man is intolerable to a fox, and any suspected approach to an earth will lead to instant removal. I appreciate this misgiving, but still am sorry that the vixen should have found it necessary to go away. My chickens are so carefully wired in that she could have brought up her family in peace. Unluckily, one can explain such things to animals even less than one can to human beings.

How often, indeed, one regrets the impossibility of coming to a reasonable understanding with the animal world. If only I could say to a conference of jays and magpies, " Look here, I will

50

gladly supply you with a daily ration of ordinary ducks' eggs, if in return you will agree to ignore the eggs of my precious Carolina ducks from whom I particularly want to breed ", all would be well. It would also be much better for the jays and magpies, since I should not then be obliged to shoot them. If I could address a labour of moles and ask them merely to refrain from tunnelling their palace under the fritillaries, giving them a free run else-where, all would again be well. They would not then have to be trapped. If I could explain to my dogs the exact area over which they might range with impunity they would then never have to be kept on a leash lest they should stray hunting on my neighbours' ground. It is all a very great pity, but how can one hope to communicate with creatures who have been denied even the gift of speech ?

Meanwhile all nature is doing her best. Everything is grow-ing, increasing, and preying on something else. Even a bantam, emulating the cuckoo, has turned a blackbird off her nest in order to use it for her own eggs. Unfortunately, the bantam being of a larger size, the nest does not fit, and the appropriation was revealed by the small omelette dropped on the ground underneath. Optimism continues to triumph. The blackbird has wisely gone off to build elsewhere. Blackbirds become remarkably bold at this time of the year. I stood watching one this morning, having its bath two yards away from me. Undisturbed by my presence, it perched on the edge of a tub, pecking at itself and shaking out its wings to the March air. It seemed to take a pride in its orange beak and glossy feathers, as though its business were to make itself as smart, clean, spring-like, male and attractive as possible. If once the blackbird recognised its inferiority in colouring to the Carolina duck whose eggs are eaten by the beauteous jay, the blackbird might well give up the struggle in competition. But as they are native not exotic birds, and as England is on the whole a sober temperate island, the blackbird still persists, even as the daffodil still persists, the Lent lily still coming up through the grasses in the orchard.

Flora

THE gardener is as busy as the vixen. His seedlings are coming up ; and to the gardener his spring flowers are as dear as her cubs to their mother. He has taken as much trouble about them, as the wild mother carrying her babies for two months in her womb ; and, even as the wild mother, he now wants to put them out into a place of safety.

Colour has crept insidiously over the garden during the last fortnight. Day by day, colour has grown. The golden curtain of the forsythia is especially splendid this year. I do not know why. I have never pruned forsythia in the way I am told to prune it, ' cut hard back to the old wood ', in the terms of horticultural wisdom. Yet never has the forsythia, the Golden Bell tree, flowered more exuberantly.

The almonds, too, are exuberant, tossing their pink sprays. A foolish snobbery puts some people against almonds. Nothing could be more mistaken than this form of snobbery which condemns some lovely flowering trees just because they happen to thrive in suburban gardens. If a tree is beautiful in itself, it retains its beauty even though it may have come into common use. Nothing can be lovelier than the blossoms of *Amygdalus communis dulcis* against the pale blue of an English March sky, unless against the deeper blue of Sicily or Greece.

Fox at Noonday

I RECENTLY observed in the correspondence columns of a daily paper a letter inquiring whether it was usual to perceive a fox approaching the habitations of man in broad daylight. I can assure the writer of the letter that a fox here, where I live, is in the habit of coming close up to the garden, where men are working, even at noonday. He is trying to catch my chickens, and his bravery is extreme. He dares the daylight, and he dares us all. The fox is usually regarded as a slinky, nocturnal animal, but this particular fox has reversed all my preconceived ideas. He must be either very hungry, or very greedy, or both. He appears at all hours and throws the poultry into hysterical consternation. The pair of guinea-fowl especially go frantic whenever the fox appears ; it is they, in fact, who give notice of his approach by their insistent cry of " Go back ! go back ! " Human vocables are often, and too imaginatively, attributed to animals and birds ; but in the case of the guinea-fowl it may justifiably be said that they really do exclaim " Go back ! go back ! " in so clear a voice as to rebuke human beings. One feels snubbed. The fox, less sensitive perhaps to such rebukes, does not feel snubbed but carries on with his marauding ways until the guinea-fowl are driven to take refuge in an oak tree. Perched on the big boughs, they chatter their " Go back ! go back ! " unheeded.

Animals certainly do behave very strangely at times, and not at all in conformity with their reputed nature. I have a swan which refuses to take to the water. I do not know whether it is a cob or a pen ; all I know is that it is one of the most sociable birds I have ever encountered, also one of the most disagreeable. Hissing with temper, flapping its great wings, it approaches whenever it sees me go out to garden, and settles down near me with an expression of intense dislike but a determination to share my company. Failing me, it sits beside the donkey. The other day it tried to follow an old gentleman into his motor car. Company it evidently must have, but with the other water-fowl sailing complacently on the moat it will have nothing to do.

The Alsatian and the Partridge

COURAGE is also a characteristic sometimes displayed in unexpected quarters. I had heard tales of a lapwing attacking a sparrow-hawk, and of a partridge's reckless bravery in the defence of her young, but never until recently had I watched the scene myself. The first indication I had was the complete and sudden rout of an Alsatian dog, whom I saw flying for refuge across a field, ears back, his tail between his legs, pursued by a small brown bird which tried to peck him as he ran. He reached me panting ; but the partridge, not yet having vented her full fury upon him, ignored my presence and continued to batter him with beak and wing. He could have crunched her into one mouthful, but making no attempt to defend himself he crouched to the ground, laughable and harassed, until I finally chased the savage little bird away. She went off to collect her chicks, but it was some time before the dog would be tempted to enter the field again.

Alsatians have a bad name and deserve it. I make this admission reluctantly, since I love the handsome pair who so vehemently and unnecessarily defend my person, my house, and my garden. I should be grateful to them for pinning down a burglar in the isolated cottage I inhabit by night, but when they leap towards the wrist of an inoffensive guest who civilly advances to shake hands with me on arrival, I feel that their enthusiasm in my defence is not only misplaced but perilous. I may have few friends, but I don't want those few to get bitten.

My guests seldom like Martin and Martha. They see them only as growling wolves that have to be kept on the leash until they have accepted the presence of the stranger. Once they have accepted it they become friendly. They will then go and rest their noses on his knee in a manner which is rather alarming after his

55

first reception. It is in vain that I explain that Alsatians are extremely sensitive dogs and that they probably wish to make amends for their initial mistake : he pats their heads with a still tentative and nervous gesture.

I am telling the truth when I say that they are sensitive. People who tell stories about their dogs are always bores, but at the risk of being a bore I must endorse the accepted belief that Alsatians are amongst the most sensitive and intelligent of dogs, especially receptive to the mood and intentions of the master. At moments they appear to be possessed of a power of telepathy unknown to most humans. Thus, although most dogs recognise the significance of luggage from force of association and realise that one is going away when they see the suit-case brought out, Alsatians are the only dogs I have ever known who sense an imminent departure even before any signs of it appear, whether in the form of luggage or unfamiliar clothes. Ears are laid back, and a black misery descends. Martha, who is the more temperamental of the two, stands shuddering from head to tail, and will not be reassured. Martin, more practical, does his utmost to escape, since he knows that my absence will mean their being shut into the kennel. How do they know ? Their knowledge can come only from the fact that in some curious way they are enabled to read my mind. And when I do return, and release them, they crowd against me and tell me whimpering stories of the anguish they have endured. These stories go on for a long time, and really seem to be a desire to express something in a speech which is denied them. It is not merely the welcome one expects from one's dog after absence ; it is a prolonged saga of sorrow which is apt to be renewed hours later whenever the dreadful memory of the separation revives.

Telepathy apart, their reasoning intelligence is also noteworthy. Thus Martin has learnt how to work the various latches on the doors. He knows that one type of latch has to be poked up by the nose, another type pressed down by the paw. He must have worked this out for himself since I have never taught him. Indeed, I would never have taught him so inconvenient a trick, which means only that I can now never shut him into any room without turning the key upon him. Martha, in spite of his example, has never learnt this trick, although in some ways more intelligent than he ; in this, as in many other instances, Alsatians are noticeably individualistic : each dog's intelligence is no guide to the special form of cleverness he will develop. I find, however, that both of them exhibit the faculty of association to a degree which would rejoice the apostles of Behaviourism. The moment they hear me put the cap on my fountain-pen they stretch and get up, knowing that that is the signal for going out. It is a tiny sound, and I have often tried to cheat them by screwing it on very silently. They are never deceived. For a long time I thought that their sense of hearing must be preternaturally acute ; I then discovered that they had also observed the preliminary gesture of taking off my spectacles.

They are thus strange dogs to deal with. The mixture of reason and emotional temperament is confusing, contradictory, and leads one to the conclusion that all Alsatian dogs ought to be severely trained and disciplined. One cannot allow a dangerous animal to think for itself beyond a certain point. One cannot allow large dogs to decide for themselves which of one's friends they will bite and which they will not bite. Such temperamental sensibility must be directed into habit-forming channels of routine, and as Alsatians adopt habits of routine very readily a good habit is as easily formed as a bad one. Train them, in fact, never to bite anyone at all. But then what are they to do when they meet the burglar ? Wag their tails and lick his hands ? To differentiate would surely be putting a strain on powers of discrimination even beyond the reach of an Alsatian.

All this is saying much about their nuisance-value but nothing about their beauty. Æsthetically, they are sharp, clean, fine. An Alsatian taking a leap over a gate is like a young athlete in perfect training ; a javelin thrower, a discobolus, an archer. For this reason, I less like to see them in the characteristic scramble over a higher obstacle ; I like the long, stream-line clear jump, and then the clean quick landing and the immediate stretching of strong limbs across the field. Alsatians seem to possess an instinctive feeling for their own decorative beauty.

A son of Martin and Martha who still has the loose legs of puppyhood, is so pale and silvery in colour that when he hangs with crossed paws out of a mullioned window, surveying the landscape, he looks like a ghost-dog mounting guard in the casement of some rose-red pre-Raphaelite manor. This habit of his is not inherited or copied from either of his parents, but is entirely his own invention. Or does it descend to him from some ancestor in the tales of the brothers Grimm ?

I rather hope that these most unprofessional notes will not attract the attention of the Alsatian League, of which I am a member.

Buying a Farm

I HAVE just bought a farm. This sounds very grand and rich and capitalistic, but I am assured by competent advisers that investment in good farming land is as sound a proposition to-day as stocks and shares. I find it very difficult to take any interest in stocks and shares, but I do find it very easy to take an interest in farm-land. It provides me with enormous pleasure to think that instead of owning some 3 per cent New Zealand Stock, which means nothing to me, I can own two hundred acres of my own county of Kent. Those two hundred acres are something tangible ; something which I can walk over and feel my own. They represent something real, not something merely set down on paper, not such dull things as New Zealand Stock or Conversion Loan. I feel then that I can say with Traherne, " When I came into the country, and being seated among silent trees and meads, and hills, had all my time in my own hands, I resolved to spend it all, whatever it cost me, in search of happiness, and to satiate that burning thirst which nature had enkindled in me from youth. In which I was so resolute, that I chose rather to live upon ten pounds a year, and to go in leather clothes, and feed upon bread and water, so that I might have all my time clearly to myself, than to keep many thousands per annum in an estate of life where my time would be devoured in care and labour."

I take an absurd pleasure in owning land. It is not for any ostentatious reason, or because I want to be a big landlord ; but simply because I love the fields and the orchards so much that I want to feel them safely mine. Safe from any builder-aggressor. Besides, the terms of the lease delight me. It delights me to read that all the hereditaments coloured pink on the map are mine ; that one-half of the soil of one-half of the bed of the stream known as the Hammer Stream is mine ; that all timber-like trees, tellers and saplings, all minerals flints gravel clay marl springs wells

and water-courses, nests, eggs, hares and wild-fowl, are mine ; that all hedges shall be properly slashed, laid, and trimmed in a workmanlike manner, nor the size or shape of any field be rendered different without my consent. All this pleases me out of all proportion, and persuades me into thinking that I live in the England of the Paston Letters.

Buying a Motor Mower

I HAVE also bought something else which pleases me far less. For many years I resisted the importation of the thing into my garden, but it has at last arrived. For a long time I am sure that my gardener suspected me of avarice : motor mowers are expensive things to buy. I think I convinced him finally of the purity of my motives when I was offered one as a free gift, and rejected it. He then thought me not stingy, but mad.

However, he has now his way. I have laid out my thirty pieces of gold and secured the enemy in exchange. Everybody on the place, except me, is delighted. They take delight in pointing out how much time the thing saves, and that one man can now do the mowing in a morning and an afternoon, whereas it used to take two men two mornings and two afternoons to do it with the old pony. I see that. But I do regret the old pony.

The old pony came here as a beautiful glossy chestnut cob. She is called Gracie Fields because she graces the fields (not *my* joke). For her weekly mowing she used to wear leather boots, which were left neatly laid out in the pattern of her feet, four chubby objects waiting beside the mower during the dinner-hour. Then would come the clank of the ancient machine as they started off again, and the summer sound of the whirring knives ; the smell of freshly cut grass as the heaps rose higher on sheets of sacking. All this has gone now, replaced by the chugging of the efficient little motor, pursued by the garden-boy walking far faster than he has ever been known to walk before and looking absurdly as though he were pushing some wild sort of pram.

There is a certain magnificence about big agricultural machinery ; even a hay-elevator has its beauty, and last year we had a hired gyro-tiller, which prowled from farm to farm and tore up the pastures with controlled and methodical savagery. The exaggeration of its massive power made it a monster of benevolent destruction ; it convulsed the clods behind it until the field looked like a choppy sea.   It has a miniature cousin, for use in gardens, which will dig a bed for you in less time than it takes to fetch the spade from the tool-shed and from which all dignity is totally lacking.   Machines, to be impressive, must either be exceedingly delicate or exceedingly large ;   there can be no half-measures ; thus the motor mower and the hand tiller are rather comic and certainly vulgar.   I do not think that my gardener has heard of the hand tiller yet, but even if he does hear of it I am determined that it shall never take its place here beside the motor mower.

Small but Vigorous

CERTAIN small animals seem to have been created with a fury of energy enough to do credit to any dictator.   On another plane of life they might have accomplished anything.   Luckily for humanity, they are limited by their size to relatively harmless activities.   One of them, indeed, the common shrew, which may be heard squeaking either with excitement or temper in the long grasses, is one of the smallest mammals in existence, but his minute framework in no way limits the ardour with which he sets about his business.   This business is usually concerned with the obtaining of food, for the shrew is one of those unfortunate creatures who must eat continuously and enormously.   It is not so much that he is greedy, as that if he neglects his appetite he simply dies.   No wonder that he is in so desperate a hurry when he knows that his last meal must be followed by another one within the hour, and that his long nose must lose no time in smelling it out.   Even at night he cannot rest, for he cannot stoke

himself up for the hours of darkness with a particularly large and late dinner : he is so constituted that he must eat often. Six times his own weight in food will see him safely round the clock, but any deprivation or delay will soon reduce him to a pathetic little corpse. If you have the time and inclination to spend most of the day hunting for worms and insects, you may keep a tame shrew and impress your friends by the readiness with which he will snatch food from your hand, but be under no delusion : this is not because he loves or trusts you, it is merely his extreme urgency leaving no room for fear.

Another hearty eater who is afflicted with a similarly precipitate temperament is that bane of gardeners, the mole. Larger and heavier than the shrew, he still demands at least the equivalent of his own weight in food each day. But consider the exercise he takes, and the violence he displays in taking it. It is enough to make anybody hungry. Semi-blind as he is, we might expect him to go about his work half-heartedly as a sluggard, but on the contrary he rushes at it as though a troop of devils were after him. Digging furiously, his track may often be watched rising in weals and mounds across the newly-raked seed-bed, tracing his progress underground. Physically the little miner is beautifully adapted for his curious mode of life ; his front paws are amazingly strong and provided with sharp claws and an extra bone ; his ears non-existent though his whole body is, one might say, an ear ; his eyes so deeply buried in his fur that they can come to no harm while he tunnels ; his fur so disposed that there is no ' wrong way ' in which it can be brushed up, a very useful asset when its owner may have to retire backwards along a narrow passage. His teeth are sharp and numerous, as you will learn if you attempt to pick him up ; his nose pointed and well designed for use as a kind of trowel ; in fact the only weak point in his whole equipment lies in the fact that he dies immediately from a rap on that useful snout.

A Model of Paternity

WHEN I was a child I used to collect sticklebacks in April and keep them in one of those square glass tanks mysteriously associated with electric light plants, first putting a few inches of sand at the bottom and some waving pond-weeds. The stickleback is an ornamental little fish, although he comes from nowhere more exotic than our native brooks and ponds : he flashes red, green, and blue as he darts in the water, bristling with the curious thorn-like weapons that give him his name and enables him to vent his rage upon other males of his species. For the stickleback, like the shrew and the mole, is small, energetic and quarrelsome. His habits are even more interesting than his appearance. He is a born father, packed with paternal love in the whole length of his three inches. His mate, in fact, is allowed no part whatsoever in the care of the offspring, beyond the sole function which he himself cannot perform.

It is he who prepares the nest, first rolling himself in the mud in the bottom of his pond or stream to scoop a suitable hollow. In this hollow he carefully builds the foundations of his nursery, which, when finished, is something like a woman's muff, as round, as neat and as cosy, but only one inch wide and with only one entrance instead of two. He has carried a lot of leaves and stringy matter to make it, and has stuck the whole thing together with a sort of liquid glue that he personally exudes, extremely busy, painstaking, and anxious. Here, however, his single-handed preparations break down. He cannot lay eggs. For this menial purpose the services of a lady have to be engaged, or perhaps we should say that the lady has to be coerced, since she shows no enthusiasm for the task but has to be fetched and piloted and even steered into the entrance. Even then she does not lay enough eggs, but has to be given two or more successors. The stickleback

65

takes no further interest in his helpers once they have done what he wanted. They are allowed to swim away and pursue their irresponsible life in the pleasant shallows. He, preoccupied, fusses round his nest, keeps a careful watch on the eggs, stirs the water softly with his fins to produce a current, and fights off any possible invader. No trouble is too great for this little model father.

One Afternoon

A T 3 p.m. I was listening to the first report of Herr Hitler's speech to the Reichstag, but by 3.30 p.m. I had gotten myself with relief out into the very different atmosphere of the open fields, the quietly busy fields, busy with their April life. Corn was springing, larks were singing, lambs and piglets being born. On my way I fell in with Henry, the man who looks to the sheep and pigs. He is a dryly ironical man with a shrewd estimation of men and animals, comforting himself always with the warm little bowl of his pipe. On this particular afternoon he invited me to accompany him to the pen where a gilt was in process of farrowing—'pigging', as Henry more realistically calls it. Three little rosy nudities had already appeared, and Henry routed out a fourth from the straw, so weak that it could scarcely stand, as he set it on its feet. Its shell-pink body faded swiftly from pink to cream, a startling transformation, as rapid as though a vein had been opened and the blood made to flow. The tiny thing became almost transparent ; wavered once ; staggered once ; fell over ; and died without a sigh. Henry, also without a sigh, threw it on to a rubbish heap. This little event of birth and death over, he began to wonder (as though he were thinking aloud to himself) how many piglets he could transfer in fostership from sow to sow : some sows produced too many, some too few ; some sows with a big litter, fourteen or fifteen, had too few ' deals ', meaning dugs ; others, the young sows, the gilts, might give birth to only three or four, and therefore might take over

67

the responsibility for more mature and prolific mothers. I listened to Henry cogitating these matters, working out his problem of supply and demand : the supply of birth-rate, the demand for food. All this took place under an orchard flushed with blossom as pink as the flesh of the healthy little new-born pigs.

He then went on to show me the sheep he had put to eat off a crop of winter-proud wheat. I was no longer really listening ; I was remembering the herdsmen of the unknown Elizabethan :

> All day their flocks each tendeth ;
> At night they take their rest ;
> More quiet than who sendeth
> His ship into the East,
> Where gold and pearl are plenty,
> But getting, very dainty.

Henry represents that herdsman to me, is a source of great pleasure, though I suspect that he sometimes regards me as a nuisance with my questions and the inexplicable interest I take in matters which to him are all in the day's work. Thus I am amused by things which to him are not amusing at all : merely an inevitable bother and interruption of his daily round. It does not seem to him in the least pleasing that one of his cows should wade across the stream on to the neighbouring farmer's meadow, leaving two distressed twin calves behind her on the other bank ; he goes about the task of getting her back, calling " Lass ! Lass ! " in a patient voice, for he knows that to show impatience towards an animal is worse than useless ; but to him there is no touching anxiety in the worried mother or the worried calves trotting up and down, unable to rejoin one another however fain they may be to do so. As I sat watching Henry at this occupation, I discerned two parallel lines of string floating on the current of the stream. Like Time, they seemed to have no beginning and no end, and I amused myself speculating on what their purpose could possibly be : were they perhaps some traditional country

form of fishing, unknown to me? If I pulled, would a net rise to the surface several fields away? I pulled gingerly, but there was no resistance and nothing but yards and yards of wet twine came into my hands. "That?" said Henry, coming back after restoring Lass to her hungry children, "That's the balls of hop-twine we put into the water upstream to shrink them, come unrolled in the floods. I shall have to ball them all up again."

So that is one of the unexpected things Henry has to do. When I remember that the twine used every year in a forty-acre hop-garden would reach from Kent to Edinburgh (so it is said) I do not wonder that he is less amused by such contretemps than I.

Now why, I often ask myself, should these ordinary things give me so deep and lasting a satisfaction ? Why should Henry's simple expressions move me more profoundly than any Dictator's rhetoric ? which, after all, is likely to affect my life and the lives of my countrymen in far greater degree. Such things cannot be set into their right proportion ; they must always return to the question of personal temperament. I sometimes think that the love of nature and the natural seasonal life may attain the proportions of a vice ; may obsess one to the extent of desiring nothing else, nothing beyond : a drowning, a lethargy, an escape, an indolence and an evasion.

Bluebells

HAD Y. Y. not stolen my thunder in *The New Statesman* last week, I should to-day be writing about the bluebells now spreading across the woods in clouds of low and horizontal smoke. They recall the smoke of autumn bonfires, only clinging to the ground instead of mounting through the trees, drifting slowly across the russet branches. Y. Y. did, however, steal my thunder very thoroughly, including an impeachment of the bluebell picker 'who comes home carrying a bunch of bluebells on his handlebar'. So I desist.

Thunder, I surmise, is not the correct word. Neither Y. Y. nor I could possibly be described as thunderous. I have met Y. Y. once only in my life, but from a constant perusal of his essays I imagine him to be a temperamentally pensive, secluded person, with tastes totally unsuited to the present day. I can imagine him very happy as the young Andrew Marvell at Appleton House, submitting patiently to the hours his tutorial duties imposed, escaping gratefully to the green shades beside the river Wharfe in his free afternoons. How deeply I find myself in agreement! The older I grow, the milder and more contemplative become my inclinations. I suppose it is because, as life becomes more and more confusing and alarming, I try to simplify it into the enduring terms I understand, which supplies the answer as to why I prefer Henry and the orchards and the cotes and all that they imply.

Eclipse

Many, if not most, people must have observed how frequently happenings occur in series. There exists a superstition that things happen in threes—you break one object and then immediately break two others, although you may not have broken anything for years. I do not know on what ground this superstition is based, but although I try (unsuccessfully) not to be superstitious, there are still certain beliefs to which I pay attention. One of those beliefs, corroborated by experience, is that although for weeks and even months one's own personal life may have remained uneventful, it will suddenly and without warning produce event after event, all in a rush, all in one day. That these events should be on a big scale or small does not affect the question. The point is, that a number of things happen suddenly within twenty-four hours. Doves enter the window at dawn and sit cooing on the window-cill; a girl gets engaged; a boy gets a job; one hears the cuckoo for the first time this spring; the swans lay eggs; two partridges are discovered to be nesting in the orchard; eighteen bantam chicks hatch out; green woodpeckers carve a hole in an apple-tree; a puppy chews the Greek tortoise, and the sun goes into eclipse.

A busy day for those who enjoy a quiet life.

The sun went gently, not dramatically, into his eclipse.

There was none of that darkened drama which attends the total phenomenon. The sun merely crept, rather cautiously on this occasion, behind the moon's shadow for three-quarters of an hour, allowing his sinking majesty to be impaired by no more than a bite out of a schoolboy's slice of bread-and-butter or the Mad Hatter's out of his teacup. It was not an impressive eclipse, as eclipses go. But even a partial eclipse, I discovered, may offer unexpected effects. I was thankful that unlike the Chilcotin Indians I need not feel obliged to tuck up my robes and, leaning on a stave, walk round in circles until the sun was once more in safety. I was thankful that I might squint simply through a smoked glass, standing outside the kitchen door, sharing the glass with other members of my small household. We passed it from hand to hand, from eye to eye. Looking westward at the sinking bitten sun, other objects came strangely into our darkened view : a flowering tree of red prunus, transmuted into a tree of a sinister loveliness unknown to any earthly botanist ; and Kentish oast-houses coming into the small dark picture too—those oast-houses which always suggest witches' hats even in ordinary daylight, but which seen through a smoked glass with an eclipse of the sun going on behind them take on an alarmingly Sabbatical character. The visiting moon did indeed leave something remarkable that day.

Evening after Eclipse

THE effect of smoky light produced by the eclipse extended itself into the starlit hours. I went out, late, and unexpectantly glanced up into the quince-tree. The ring-doves who had sat cooing on my window-cill early in the morning were now roosting in the quince, their feathers dappled by starlight ; the leaves of the quince were dappled by starlight too. The stars of heaven were bright beyond. The leaves were as sharply defined as in an

Umbrian landscape by Perugino. I could not have believed, and do not expect anyone else to believe, how lovely were the doves, the leaves, and the stars. It was one of those visions which one will never forget but can never hope to communicate to anyone who has not seen the same thing at the same moment with the same eyes; a rare moment, a rare vision, unshared, private, and precious.

Meanwhile, the romance of the betrothed girl was going on; the excitement of the boy with his new job; the majestic calm of the swans taking turns on their nest; and the pain of the little Greek tortoise with his shell bleeding where the puppy had chewed it. Evening sank. The sun had disappeared beyond the horizon in an eclipse greater than the nibble of eclipse he had suffered earlier in the evening. Night sank. Peace came.

Then the warrior searchlights started to joust in the sky.

May

AT this season of the year, when so much in nature happens so quickly, I find it difficult to keep my head. I surmise that such a phrase may read as an affectation ; yet I protest with all my sincerity that I do try to set down on paper as simply and directly as possible the feelings by which I am moved. It is a hard thing to do ; hard not to appear either exaggerated or mawkish, precious or inexact. It is very difficult indeed to write about nature and the natural processes without getting bogged in morasses of sentimental language. It is difficult for any honest writer to express his feelings in a way which will convince himself, let alone his readers, of his original sincerity ; and if it is hard enough to be starkly honest towards ourselves even in our own private thoughts, to arrive without embellishment or gloss at what we really mean, the writer alone knows how far harder it is to be faithful on paper. Something comes between the writer and his pen ; the passionate feeling, the urgency to record, emerge as a blob of ink, a smudge, a decoration. As Orlando discovered, green in nature is one thing, green in literature another. Thus if I set down that I have to-day seen apple-blossom strewn by wind on grass, I am stating a fact, and if I should happen to re-read my own words in future years (which is unlikely) they will probably recall that vision, as fresh and bright in memory as on that morning in the month of May. If, on the other hand, I start to expand my statement, in the hope of evoking a similar vision in the mind's eye of another, I shall immediately find myself drawn into semi-falsities, into truth wrapped round with untruth ; I shall immediately begin to search for what the apple-blossom was ' like ' ; I shall find confetti or snowflakes as a convenient comparison ; I shall hit on the word shell-pink to express the delicacy, the papery delicacy of the scattered petals ;

I shall begin to ' write ' ; but really, if I can be sufficiently severe
with myself, I shall put my pen through all those blobs of ink,
those wordy words, and cut myself back to the short phrase about
apple-blossom strewn by wind on grass. It ought to be evocative
enough, without amplification ; but such is the impuissance of
the human mind that it requires expansion before the experience
of one person can be communicated to another. Or, at any rate,
it requires a magic which mere prose is unable to provide. This is
where poetry comes in ; where poetry is, or should be, so far more
evocative, more suggestive, than prose. Prose is a poor thing, a
poor inadequate thing, compared with poetry which says so much
more in shorter time.

Writing is indeed a strange and difficult profession.

Farmers and Beauty

IN this connexion I have a quarrel with Dr. Joad. To me, he is not the distinguished lecturer of Birkbeck College, or even C. E. M. Joad, but simply Cyril, a puzzled philosopher trying to arrange the complications of life to suit his own ideas—an impossible attempt. My friend Cyril, then, who blows in on me occasionally with a knapsack on his back—for he is a confirmed hiker—writes several books every year and contrives to enrage me in each one. In his latest work he makes some remarks which I must challenge. He knows no farmer, he says, who cares for beauty. The English country-side, he says, is admittedly very beautiful, but who finds it to be so? The townsman. It is, he says, the townsman rather than the countryman who sensitively perceives the country. Pressing his argument, he instances Shakespeare, Richard Jefferies, and W. H. Hudson as writers on nature who have spent most of their lives in towns ; in fact he goes so far as to call them townsmen, which they certainly never were by origin, but only in later life. I quarrel with him on all these points.

My experience of farmers (and labourers, too) is that many have a deep though inarticulate appreciation of the beauty of nature. They may not be endowed with Joad's gift of expression, but the silent contentment they bring to the smoking of their evening pipe as they lean over a gate when the day's work is done, surveying a clean orchard or a good crop coming up, is at least as deep as Joad's who has not had the bother, sweat, risk, and expense of spraying the orchard or sowing the crop. I deny absolutely that the countryman has no sense of the beauty he has himself (inadvertently and centennially) created. Of course he takes a more practical view than Joad. He surveys his acres with an eye to caterpillars, weevils, and weeds. That does not imply blindness

77

to the beauty of his landscape.   It implies only that Joad-in-the-
country has nothing to do but to observe the landscape and think
of his next book, whereas the countryman in his rare hour of
leisure has the double job of enjoying his acres and of wondering
whether he has done the best he can by them for their own
benefit and his own necessary profit.   I freely admit that the real
countryman's enjoyment of beauty may not be ' pure ' ;   it is
associated with cognisant reflections ;   less detached than that of
the townsman who stands outside it ;   more intimately connected ;
it represents the difference, let us say, between marriage and
romance.   What Joad overlooks, however, is that marriage and
romance are not necessarily disparate.

Fishing

O<small>N</small> a calm, warm evening with bats and flies about, just the happy sort of evening to pull a trout towards sunset out of the lake, I went down hopefully equipped with rod and landing-net ; took out the boat ; and found myself confronted by a large wet sheep.

The poor thing had been driven into the water by a dog—my own dog, suddenly gone gay. Fortunately it was also one of my own sheep, one of that unusual horned variety known as Jacob's sheep, so that I need feel no sense of guilt or apprehension towards an injured farmer. I did, however, feel a sense of responsibility towards the animal itself and rowed towards it in a spirit of rescue, discovering then (not for the first time) how very difficult it is to help animals in distress, so profound and instinctive is their mistrust of one's good intentions. Alarmed by my approach it made efforts to swim, and indeed did very nobly as a swimmer, crossing the lake as I rowed after it, swimming desperately in the effort to escape me whom it took to be yet another enemy. I caught it up on the farther shore, where it stuck in the shallows, enabling me to lasso it neatly round the horns with the boat's painter ; I had no other rope, so had to sacrifice the painter with my knife. We sat contemplating one another, the sheep and I, I still wishing to fish but entangled instead with this poor tiresome creature, unwillingly looped to it by a rope, faced by the need of getting it safely back to land. It looked at me with vacant eyes ; seldom had I seen so unhelpful a victim. We stared at one another, and as we stared it sank lower and lower, getting wetter and wetter, until its fleece billowed out like a Victorian bathing-dress filling with water, floating on the surface in woolly flounces half buoyant, half sodden. Its long tail drifted on the surface behind it, an absurd sausage. I tugged at the rope hoping to tow it back to shore, but

79

the beast, apparently intent on frustrating my friendly purpose, wrapped its forelegs round a stump of old willow and could not or would not be budged. I sat back in the boat thinking how ticklish a problem it was ever to help people out of their private difficulties, the sheep meanwhile continuing to contemplate me with the same vacant unhelpful eyes. I tugged again ; rolled up my sleeve ; sank my arm to the elbow ; grasped the all too muscular forelegs ; succeeded in unwinding them from the stump ; and eventually rowed off with the sheep in tow, a ludicrous rodeo that ended in landing the most unexpected fish I ever caught.

More Fishing

YEARS ago, in Scotland, I used to fish far more successfully. I think the trout there must have been less sophisticated ; they certainly showed more willingness to be caught ; and as I never found a half-drowned sheep waiting for me in the loch, my attempts at fishing were uninterrupted. I could always be certain of bringing back five or six trout for breakfast on the following morning. I shall never forget the enchantment of those evenings —the walk up to the loch, alone or with my father, the loosening of the small moored boat, the paddling out into the platter of still water surrounded by heather hills, the silence, the privacy, the soft dip of the oars, the soft swish of the cast, the stillness, the sudden rush of the line, the rasp of the reel, the rush of the fish, the excitement of waiting with landing-net poised, the gleam of the tired fish coming to the surface almost ready to be scooped out of the water yet with enough life left in him to make one last dash, the beauty of the hills all around us, the final successful scoop, the twitching speckled body dropped in the bottom of the boat. My father was a humane man, but neither he nor I could resist the

zeal of that brief intense struggle with a prey so far colder and smaller than ourselves. I have observed that humanitarianism is deplorably apt to work in ratio to the size and charm of the victim concerned. Thus although my father had no objection to catching trout, nothing would induce him to shoot the roe-deer in the woods. Once or twice during the season there were organised beats which he hated but never had the moral courage to forbid. He would take me with him, and together we would stand waiting in a clearing, he with his gun ready and an unspoken understanding between us of what he meant to do. We both liked the woods ; we liked the sounds, the bracken, the birches ; we never talked much ; even the dogs stayed quiet ; our own quietness seemed to influence them. Then from a distance would come the noise of the beaters advancing, and suddenly a smaller noise—the crack of a twig, the rustling of a leaf—a frightened little noise, the tremble of a fugitive. An interval of silence always seemed to impose itself between the advance of the beaters and the forerunners of the deer ; some moments of suspense during which the deer and the man with the gun were intimately and fatally connected. They came in terror, and he waited, the murderer filled with secret mercy. Peering round a tree-trunk came the first elegant little head, the bright eyes, the tiny horns, the active arrested hooves, searching for escape down the familiar ways. Nimbleness paused and peered. Then he, taking apparently careful aim, would fire and a scamper of feet would follow. How had he managed to miss ? The fruitless report must have scared all deer for a mile round. Yet he was generally considered as a very good shot.

Shooting

HE did not like big covert drives either, though as a good shot he was always invited to them, and again owing to a lack of moral courage he seldom refused. Propped on our shooting-sticks, he and I would wait at the edge of a wood, beside the split rod fluttering a bit of rag to mark his standing. On those richly golden autumnal afternoons, with his loader and dog, we must have looked like a photograph in the social illustrated papers. I do not think he enjoyed it any more than I did. There was an excitement, of course, as the birds began to come over, and a certain satisfaction as the big pheasant suddenly crumpled in the air, falling with a thud a few yards away ; but he always called it slaughter and would flick the blood from the breast feathers with a regretful finger. What he really enjoyed was rough shooting, where he felt that he and the birds stood a more even chance ; he felt that these were wild birds, not fat semi-tame things expensively bred for the fashionable sportsman's pleasure ; besides, a tramp of ten or fifteen miles over rough ground and through wet turnips helped to justify the few brace he could carry home in his own (and my) pockets. To this day I can feel the cold wetness of the ' roots ' sloshing round my ankles, then the drying brush of the heather. His dog and I followed him in equal obedience. We never knew if we were going to put up a partridge, a pheasant, a woodcock, a snipe, or even a grouse. The element of chance and difficulty swept all those covert-shooting days from our souls like a clean wind. We had no loader with us then, no keeper expecting a five-pound tip ; freedom was ours and the sporting chance.

He was a pleasing man, my father.

Other People's Gardens

THERE exists, as most persons interested in such matters have by now discovered, an imaginative and well-organised scheme which enables us to visit other people's gardens. In the old days we used to peer wistfully over a hedge, allured by some gay border, some group of flowering shrubs, wishing with all our heart that we might penetrate further and wander unhurried and unescorted through the suggestive revelation of somebody else's ideas. Nothing but a shrinking from the thought of intrusion prevented us from ringing the front-door bell and asking for the necessary permission, no doubt gladly to be granted, since all true gardeners are friendly, generous, ungrudging people. Now, all that is changed. Our longing need no longer be thwarted, even by our own delicacy. In return for one silver shilling laid down on a table we have the freedom of the most beautiful gardens in England, magnificent and modest alike. In return for one shilling we are made citizens of the most lovely, private, and idealistic of boroughs—the gardener's own intimate familiar home.

We have been called a nation of shopkeepers ; we might with equal justice be called a nation of gardeners. The membership-roll of the Royal Horticultural Society climbs towards forty thousand, a figure which may not rival the Tail-Waggers, who have now passed the half-million mark ; still, taking the two societies together, gardeners and dog-lovers, the figures must surely represent something essentially peaceful and amiable in our national life. A nation that so profoundly and extensively loves flowers and dogs must surely have something very unbellicose in its make-up. I remember once attending a flower-show in Berlin, where the principal exhibit was of the most spiky and truculent forms of cactus, grey-green bayonets, murderous pikes—a horrid symbol, I thought, at the time, although that was more than ten years ago and the Führer's name only an insignificant whisper. The second principal exhibit was an avenue of tombstones, appropriately decorated with wreaths or bouquets of tin flowers. In a flash I saw English cottage gardens ; I saw the fortnightly shows at Vincent Square ; the dove-coloured spinsters coming up from the country with their little note-books, peering closely down into the mealy auriculas, taking notes, placing their orders rather cautiously since they could not afford to be unduly extravagant and must cogitate longly over even a sixpenny packet of seed ; then lingering over the flaming azaleas, the rose-red prunus, all so enticing ; and then the *sotto voce* conversations : " But you know, my dear, one can't *trust* these nurserymen ; they tell you something is perfectly hardy when of course it isn't, except perhaps in Devonshire, and anyhow one knows they bring things on under glass, so how can one order things happily to try out in one's own garden ? " So, worried and dubious, they go round the halls at Vincent Square ; but at any rate they are dealing with real possible flowers, not with the sinister cacti and mortuary wreaths of the Berlin equivalent of our Chelsea show.

This worry and dubiousness is naturally removed when you go round somebody else's garden. No fake is possible there : you see things growing in the open where they have always grown. There is no question of not trusting the nurseryman, or of things having been grown for a specific purpose under glass. This is the main difference between the garden and the show. In the garden you see things growing as they have grown in their natural way, taking their chance of frost, wind, and rain. No spurious advantage has been brought to it except the love and green fingers of the owner.

It is a real experience to open one's garden to the public. In a sense you might think it a desecration, a violation of one's patch of private peace. ' How offensive ', you might think, ' to have eight hundred strangers straggling all over one's very personal property ! ' You would be wrong. It is a pleasure ; even a form

of flattery. It removes all sense of guilty egoistic pleasure. You
share your personal delight ; the scheme you have built up for
ten, twenty years becomes part of the pleasure of hundreds of
inquisitive eager gardeners, makers of beauty. It is very necessary
to have makers of beauty left in a world seemingly bent on making
the most evil ugliness. These mild, gentle men and women who
invade one's garden after putting their silver token into the bowl,
these true peace-makers, these inoffensive lovers of nature in her
gayest form, these homely souls who will travel fifty miles by bus
with a fox-terrier on a lead, who will pore over a label, taking
notes in a penny note-book—those are some of the people I most
gladly welcome and salute. Between them and myself a particular
form of courtesy survives, a gardener's courtesy, in a world where
courtesy is giving place to rougher things.

Other People's Ideas

Seeing other people's gardens in this way with the consent and encouragement of their owners is not only agreeable but valuable. Other people's ideas always seem better than, perhaps only because they are different from, one's own. I have some definite ideas about gardening myself—for example, I believe in exaggeration ; I believe in big groups, big masses ; I am sure that it is more effective to plant twelve tulips together than to split them into two groups of six ; more effective to concentrate all the delphiniums into one bed, than to dot them about at intervals of twos and threes. I believe also in picking up the hints that nature gives us, and in taking full exaggerated use of them, seizing on the chance effects of plant-association. For instance I once grew catmint right along the top of a retaining wall, and that was pretty enough, but then one day a seedling of the Cheddar pink appeared just in front of the catmint, and the little rosy flowers of the pink mixed themselves so suitably with the mauve sprays of the catmint that I sowed more Cheddar pink the whole way along the top of the wall in front of the mint, with the result that in the following year I had a misty mingling of pink and mauve which I should never have thought of, if that seedling had not shown me the way to do it. Apart from the flowers, the grey-green sprays of the catmint and the grey-green lumps of the pink made a quiet combination even when neither plant was in flower. It was satisfactory the whole year round, summer and winter.

Then another day I noticed that a blue gentian, *sino-ornata*, had wandered from the place where it was meant to be, and had set itself just in front of a bush of blue plumbago. The gentian and the plumbago were in full flower at the same time, and I saw that if one wanted to produce the effect that a piece of the best blue sky had fallen down to earth, one must plant *Ceratostigma*

89

Willmottiana with the gentian all round its feet. Near by, the forget-me-not Royal Blue was struggling up through the mauve wallflower *Cheiranthus linifolium*. The possibilities are endless. I never thought of setting the blue poppy under the swags of *Rosa Moyesii*, till a stray poppy gave me the hint. Escallonia Donard's seedling flowered suddenly one year behind a large clump of Iris Quaker Lady. The small pink violet (I think it is Cœur d'Alsace) crawled over to a group of *Iris reticulata*, another hint which should be taken.

These were the cool-coloured, but I also have in mind a long double border, enclosed between dark hedges, carried out in a scheme of red, orange, and yellow that looked hot and sunny even on a grey day. There was a paved walk right down the middle, and on either side grew this fiery profusion of red and orange snapdragons and dahlias, velvety red salpiglossis, eschscholtzias in every shade from yellow to flame, zinnias like balls of fire, and a great clump of red-hot pokers towering in torches at one end. The scarlet *Verbena chamœdryoides* trailed over the paved walk lying very flat and pressed on the grey stones. Someone had evidently spilt a packet of snapdragon seeds by mistake, and it had germinated in the cracks of the paving, making a sudden lake of blood-red in the middle of the path.

The same idea was repeated earlier in the year in a little square garden, entirely enclosed by a hedge of rosemary. There were Iceland poppies of the most brilliant shade of orange ; Siberian wallflower ; yellow alyssum ; and that best of all orange roses, Mrs. G. A. van Rossem, mixed with that amazingly flame-coloured rose, Dazzler. The common little golden sedum had dumped itself in tiny cushions all over the paths. The real touch of genius came in a huge spray of the tall Austrian copper briar, flinging its gold and orange fountains over the smaller things growing at its feet. Single, like all the briars, it threw itself about in a wild exuberance, ten or twelve feet high ; coppery in colour, red on the inside of the petals and yellow on the outside,

brilliant with the brilliance of a nasturtium.   It was a fine lesson
in the art of not mixing one's manners ;   a bold experiment,
wholly successful.

Then I remember a herb-garden, planned on a tiny scale ;
put into terms of an ordinary room, I don't suppose that it would
occupy more than the ordinary floor-space.   And everything in it
was exactly to scale ;   the paths were only two-bricks wide, the
middle was occupied by a tiny stone column, there were four

beds each no bigger than a wide-spread table-cloth, and yet they seemed to be packed with all the herbs that the most exacting French cook could possibly desire.

There is one sort of garden which I much want to possess. It is an Alpine lawn. Those who have walked over the Alpine pastures know how the small, bright flowers of those regions grow in the short turf, the little violas and pinks and gentians, orchises and harebells, all blowing together over miles of upland. I want to reproduce this effect on a small scale. But my lawn would not be given turf as its foundation, for in this country the grass would grow too long, and the presence of the flowers would make mowing an impossibility. It would be composed of thyme, the densest and most creeping sort, and before I laid the thyme I should set whatever plants I wanted, choosing those which would not object to this dense mass growing round them. *Gentiana verna*, for instance, would revel in it, and what could be lovelier than the brilliant blue of its trumpets coming through the dark green of the thyme ? Then I should have bulbs—scillas, and grape hyacinths, and crocus, and some of the miniature narcissus, and those very small Persian and Greek tulips, linifolia and orphanidea. I should make this glorified toy symmetrical, either square or rectangular according to the shape of the piece of ground, and at the four corners I should plant four very straight little trees of the John Downie crab-apple, for in the autumn, when the flowers had disappeared, the sealing-wax fruits would hang as in a Mantegna or a Crivelli above the dark cloth of thyme.

I suppose that one must have an edging to keep the thyme within bounds, and I should like to make it of grey stone slabs placed on edge, not more than four or five inches high. One might allow *Raoulia subserica* to crawl over some of the stones.

Stone Troughs

TROUGH-GARDENING has recently become popular, and there is much to be said in its favour. Trough-gardening means using old stone pig-troughs and stone sinks for growing plants so tiny and delicate that they might escape notice in the open garden. The principal advantage of these troughs or sinks is that they may easily be raised to eye-level on supports of brick or stone, so that their contents may be appraised without undue stooping or peering ; they are, so to speak, a garden in miniature adapted to the needs of the short-sighted or of those afflicted by rheumatism or lumbago. Even for the strong-bodied gardener they have their uses. They enable him to grow his choice small things in pockets of soil especially adapted to their needs. He can place them in sun or shade ; he can supply or withhold water as they require ; he can watch and supervise ; he can perceive the alien weed and remove it in its seedless babyhood. It is a very intimate and myopic form of garden pleasure.

These troughs or sinks are not difficult to obtain nowadays. Galvanised iron has superseded the drinking-troughs in the fields, and glazed china in the scullery sinks. Many of them have been thrown away as useless, or turned upside down to form a doorstep. I myself possess a trough which I found lying in a pig-sty, and which I discovered was traditionally known as Wat Tyler's foot-bath, having been bought under that description from his old home. It is now filled with small bright blue flowers—gentians, lithospermum, and *Omphalodes lucillæ* : Wat Tyler certainly never intended it for such a purpose, even if he did use it as a foot-bath, which I doubt ; but the gain equally certainly is mine.

The Chelsea Flower Show

THE worst of the Chelsea Show, from the reporter's point of view, is that there is nothing to say about it. It is perfection —the gardener's dream come true. One may complain that the tents are too hot, or too wet, or that there are too many people, but at least one cannot complain that there are too few plants or that the exhibitors have not done their job superbly. Their job is to produce the most exquisite flowers most magnificently grown, and no one can say that they fail to carry out their obligation. The rest is beyond their control.

One grievance commonly expressed by the casual visitor is that ' the Show is always the same '. This is true, and yet not quite true. Of course, the old favourites are there and always will be, in such array that the novelties are apt to get overlooked amongst them. Yet there have always been ' sensations ', and still are. It was only last year that we first saw the Russell lupins in their extraordinary variety of colour, so far removed from the old familiar blue as to seem almost a different flower. Going further back, there was the day when Rhododendron Pink Pearl startled everybody from Queen Alexandra downwards ; the day when the blue poppy made its first appearance ; and that other day when an exhibit of gigantic pansies provoked an old gardener into saying : " Them's not pansies ; them's lies."

In 1938 in particular there were a lot of lies. The snap-dragons had turned into church spires, the delphiniums into cathedral towers, the bougainvilleas into flaming sunsets bearing no resemblance to the old magenta curtains we used to know. Some of the lilies, competing with Jack's beanstalk, had shot up to such a height that one could view them comfortably only from a distance. In amongst these monstrous growths crept the usual crowd of keen amateur gardeners, so keen, so amateur, so touching

94

in their raincoats, with their note-books and pencils in hand. I thought they seemed a little dwarfed and humbled before this amazing display of the craft they modestly attempted to practise in their own gardens.

It may be ungrateful to criticise, especially when people have taken so much trouble, but does one really like the amazing results that the nurserymen have been able to produce? I think the answer divides itself sharply into two parts. One likes and welcomes the advances made by experiments in hybridisation, which lead to really new beauties among, say, the lupins, the irises, or the primulas. One positively dislikes the mere triumphs of scientific feeding which lead only to an appalling turgescence among our old familiar friends the cottage-garden flowers. I never believed I could be frightened by a snapdragon until I went to the Chelsea Show.

Besides, one knows quite well that, even given the desire, one could never reproduce the same effect in one's own garden. Not without taking continuous trouble or without employing a number of very painstaking and very expensive gardeners, all provided with sacks or bottles full of the most expensively specialised fertilisers. Few of us can afford such luxuries, and even if we could afford them I doubt whether the most sincere flower-lovers amongst us would wholly appreciate the results of their efforts. I think that inside our hearts we all prefer the old flowers as we have usually known them. We are alarmed, and somewhat humiliated, by the overfed unnatural specimens misleadingly staged for our benefit at the Chelsea Show. The exhibitors are not to blame: they are only carrying out their job with all the resources now at their disposal. But the rest of us cannot emulate them, and many of us would not wish to do so.

Gardens &
Gardeners

I MYSELF took to gardening quite late in life. I must have been at least twenty-two. As a child at home, I had always had a strip which was known as 'Vita's garden', because of the tradition that every child must automatically love and cherish a garden of its own, but in point of fact I didn't and furthermore it wasn't really my garden at all. For one thing, it is a complete fallacy to believe that any but the most exceptional child enjoys so peaceful a pastime as weeding, watering, and generally caring for the welfare of the patch with which it has been entrusted : the average child is far too unmethodical and far too impatient. Weeds grow too fast and flowers too slowly. Waiting for weeks and even months for your seeds or bulbs to come into bloom seems like waiting for years at a tender age. Meanwhile the weeds grow apace, and you regard with distaste the task of pulling them up, especially when it is suggested to you by your elders. It is much more fun to grow mustard and cress on damp flannel on the schoolroom window-sill. You can sow it in the shape of your own initials ; it comes up within a very few days ; and then you can eat it for tea. Very satisfactory.

Thus it came about that whenever my garden showed signs of becoming an eyesore and a wilderness, a company of gardeners would arrive with hoes, forks, and rakes, and speedily restore it to order. Thus, also, I very naturally lost any personal interest in it ; any personal interest, that is to say, which I might ever have had. If the gardeners looked after it, why should I ? It was only when I grew up, and had a house and garden of my own, that I discovered the delights and pains of gardening for myself.

As a child I had the good fortune to live in an exceptionally beautiful home, with acres of garden to match, all enclosed within a high stone wall. There were wide expanses of green lawn ; miles (as it seemed to me) of flower-borders ; little orchards here and there ; and a wilder part full of tall trees, mossy paths, and a carpet of bluebells. Of course, such a garden had to be kept orderly and trim, and my own little patch could not be allowed to offend. The head-gardener was the terror of my life. He was an immensely dignified man, with a hooked nose, keen eyes, and a great black beard, giving him the appearance of a major prophet. From time to time he used to descend on me with accusations of having robbed his peach trees or destroyed his borders by picking flowers, accusations which were sometimes well founded and sometimes not. In those days I regarded him as an ogre and a spoil-sport, but looking back on him now I see that he was merely a typical head-gardener of the grander sort, justly exasperated by the depredations of an irresponsible child. Absolute lord in his own domain, he must have counted me among the worst of his garden-pests.

I can look back on him now with affection and respect. His family had been in the service of mine for several generations. He was a fine traditional type of man, complete with his virtues and his faults. His virtues were many, including a great pride in the place, which I think he considered more as his own property than my grandfather's or my father's. His majestic appearance was enhanced by the green baize apron which he always wore on weekdays ; it seemed to set him apart from other men ; and oddly emphasised by the strand of raffia which he always carried twisted round his ear. He had some charming little habits, too ; for instance, he would send in a solitary apple or pear, the first

of the season, a label with its name carefully tied to its stalk, to be placed before my father's plate at luncheon. Invariably, also, a slip of paper recording the temperature was laid on my father's plate at breakfast : Min. 40°, Max. 60°. When I was young it never occurred to me to ask who Min and Max might be ; I simply accepted them as people who lived in the garden.

On Sundays he discarded the green baize apron, and appeared dressed in funereal black with his whole family in church.

His faults, I regret to say, were also many. They proceeded from no vice inherent in his nature (for he was an upright man), but from sheer obstinacy and a dislike of changing anything to which he had grown accustomed. He thus disliked cutting vegetables while they were still fit to use and preferred to let them run to seed rather than allow them to be delivered young and succulent into the kitchen. This, I have since found, is a failing common to nearly all professional gardeners. Then, of course, when it came to the flower garden, he had no taste at all. He grew, and grew very skilfully, the most hideous and ill-assorted plants with no regard whatsoever for colour, suitability, or elegance. Such a thing as a colour-scheme had never entered his mind ; nor, so long as he could keep his health and his job, would it be allowed to enter it. Every now and then my father, spurred on by some gardening friend, would make a protest ; but although the black-bearded prophet would listen respectfully and politely, it never made any difference to the garden. Things went on in exactly the same way as before.

I greatly preferred his second-in-command, a gentle timid little man who had a real feeling for flowers, and who was far too weak to be in command at all, even as second. He and I were friends, not enemies. He explained to me so wistfully why he minded my cutting the delphiniums he had just spent hours in staking, that I felt ashamed of my thoughtlessness. He never scolded, he only pleaded. So I listened, instead of trying to outwit him. Under the right guidance, that man could have been turned into a true and sensitive gardener. He was excessively nervous, and kept touching his cap at every sentence while he talked to one. It was a trick, a habit, which was generally attributed to the fact that he had somehow managed to collect a bullet lodged in his brain. Nevertheless, he was a born gardener, and a little enterprise and encouragement from above would have transformed him from a drudge into a creator.

Unfortunately, this brand of encouragement was seldom forthcoming from the old-fashioned head-gardener fixed in his grooves. He was so temperamentally opposed to any innovations that the apprentice under his rule had no chance whatever to enlarge his ideas or to experiment with them. Yet, actually, gardening fashions were rapidly changing under the example of certain pioneers, who not only grew plants in unorthodox ways, but also reintroduced many old favourites which had been forgotten. They were doing things calculated to horrify the head-gardeners of my acquaintance. They wished entirely to scrap the old bedding-out system, which meant the abolition of such plants as lobelias, begonias, and calceolarias, dear to the heart of gardeners of the Victorian generation. Instead of this system (which entailed much trouble as well as producing a hideous and stereotyped result), they advocated the planting of charming old perennials, with some regard to colour, design, and flowering season. They even suggested that separate parts of the garden should be set aside for seasonal beauty, discarding the old idea that every part of the garden should show some colour, however sparsely, at every time of the year. These ideas were very revolutionary, and took a long time to penetrate the armour of the professional paid gardener ; in fact, I doubt if they have generally penetrated it to this day. It is only by insistence that the well-informed employer can get what he wants done in his garden.

Yet there can be no doubt that gardening is a real and widespread passion among the English people. You have only to

One petal cannot grow without the benefit of the flowers in general nourishment.

motor through country districts, to observe that every little cottage
has its front garden overflowing with flowers. You have only to
attend one of the fortnightly flower-shows held by the Royal
Horticultural Society at their own hall in London, to see the
numbers of serious, amateur gardeners poring intently over even
the tiniest exhibit. It is no social function, this fortnightly show ;
it exists solely for the true lovers of flowers ; it is in no way
comparable to the great Chelsea Show, from which many of the
true flower-lovers abstain, because they contend (and rightly)
that they cannot get near the flowers, and are not interested in
the fashionable world which flocks to the Show with no more
interest in the flowers than they will later display in the race-
horses when in due course they flock to Ascot. Again, you have
only to knock at the front door of any little manor house, to be
greeted by a puzzled interrupted lady in a large straw hat, a pair of
leather gloves, and a trowel in her hand, whom you have disturbed
in the act of planting out her stocks. When she has recovered
from her surprise, she will be only too pleased to lead you
intimately round her garden.

That is the way in which the English love their gardens, not
because it is ' the right thing ' to do, but because it is in their
blood, from the cottager to the lady of the manor.

Again, you have only to visit some settlement abroad, when
you will find that round every little shanty or bungalow the
English occupier has endeavoured to scrape a garden from the
hopeless soil. Stony, sun-baked, waterless it may be, but still a
few petunias or snapdragons struggle for existence, carefully
tended by the tired man in his shirt-sleeves. It is really touching,
sometimes, to come across these pitiable efforts in unlikely places.
The exile cannot live without his handful of flowers to remind
him of home.

Nevertheless, as I have said, despite this ruling passion, it
took a long time for certain novel ideas to reach either the salaried
gardener or even his employer. At the beginning of the nineteenth

century, when romanticism was so much in vogue, a considerable
change had been worked by the so-called ' landscape gardening '
introduced by Capability Brown and others, who aspired to
banish formality in favour of ' nature '. This they attempted to
do by transforming straight paths into winding ones ; by planting
conifers and dark, dank shrubs at the edges of lawns ; even by
building sham ruins in the Gothic style which might serve as
summer-houses or as objects of interest at the end of a vista.
Landscape gardening when boldly carried out on an extensive
scale was sometimes successful, but when reproduced in miniature
it led only to a shapeless, meaningless disaster. The result was
then neither a garden nor ' nature '.

Curiously enough, also, the landscape idea was seldom pushed
up to the walls of the house itself. Around the house the theory
of formal beds persisted ; it was only when you wandered a
little distance away that you were supposed to find nature
unfolding herself in serpentine paths and sinister shrubberies of
laurel and rhododendron. " The ugliness of the garden about
the house," it has been well said, " was assumed to be an essential
part of the thing itself, removing that for ever from the sympathies
of artistic people. The flower-garden planting was made up of
a few kinds of flowers which people were proud to put out in
thousands and tens of thousands, and with these, patterns, more
or less elaborate, were carried out in every garden save the very
poorest cottage garden." There could be no truer description.
Left to the professional working-gardener, the beds were regularly
filled year after year with scarlet geraniums, pink begonias,
discordant salvias, yellow calceolarias, and greenhouse plants with
variegated foliage. Nothing more hideous, unsuitable, or unnatural
could be imagined. The beds themselves, which were usually
set in lawns, were of equally unpleasing shape, either kidney,
heart, or lozenge, which perhaps was just as well, as it matched
the planting-scheme and it was better that the gardener should
be hanged eventually for a sheep than for a lamb.

So frightful was the whole arrangement, in fact, that some
enterprising spirits began to feel that it could be borne no longer.
There was something wrong with gardening, but what? And
where was the remedy to be found? The words which I quoted
a few lines back were written in 1883 by a man to whom
gardeners owe all possible gratitude and honour. In his own
profession he was one of the most remarkable men I have ever
known, and his career and achievement were no less remarkable
than his personality.

Of the earlier part of his life I can speak only by hearsay. I am given to understand that he was born of the humblest parentage, and that he started on his career as a garden-boy. When I first met him, he was a very old man, nearing eighty if, indeed, he had not passed it, totally paralysed, and extremely rich. Exactly how he had managed to amass his fortune between the days when he was a poor little boy sweeping up leaves for the wage of a few shillings a week, and the days when I came to know him as the owner of an Elizabethan house and one of the loveliest gardens in England, I have never been able to discover. I know that he had gradually worked his way upward ; I know also that he had made a name for himself as a designer of gardens ; that he founded at least two popular gardening papers ; and that (among several other books) he had written one called *The English Flower Garden*, which to this day remains a classic in horticultural literature. Still, all this does not seem sufficient to account for the enormous difference between his early fortunes and his later. I do not seek to explain it, nor to pry into his private life by asking questions of friends who knew him far better than I ever did : such inquisitiveness would be merely impertinence. I am quite content to rest with the memory of the courteous old man I saw in his invalid-chair, sitting out in the sun among his flowers, unable to raise his head, scarcely able to move his hands, but still sufficiently alert to take pride in the garden he had created and to talk with knowledge and enthusiasm about his schemes and his innovations.

After luncheon, I well remember, he announced that he would like to take me all through his woods. I was somewhat appalled by this suggestion, as I failed to see how this helpless paralytic could possibly be propelled all over the acres of his estate, especially by rough woodland paths, for I was unprepared for what was to follow. At a signal, four sturdy men appeared, and, heaving their master bodily out of his chair, dumped him in a motor-car furnished with caterpillar wheels. He invited me to take my place beside him and off we went. It was my first experience of such a tank-like machine, and I confess that seldom have I been more alarmed. We lurched, we heaved, we threatened to turn over, we crossed swamps, we climbed banks, we ascended hills almost vertically, we descended hills clinging on to the sides of the car to prevent ourselves from being shot forward. I kept a nervous eye on what was coming next, but my host, well wrapped up in his blankets, appeared to be quite unmoved. He talked learnedly all the time about blue spruces and I daresay about other spruces also, but I was in no state of mind to profit by these remarks. He was justly proud of his woods, but personally I was relieved when we returned to the nice, flat, flagged paths of his garden.

He was an admirable old man, was William Robinson, and I suppose he did more to alter the fashions of English gardening than any man of his time, not excepting such worthy contemporaries as Miss Gertrude Jekyll. The quotation which I gave from one of Mr. Robinson's prefaces shows that as long ago as 1883 he had grown discontented with the fashions he described as then in vogue. His preoccupation was what to substitute for them. Luckily for him and for us, he had occasion to wander round the countryside and to observe for himself how charming and withal simple were the happy-go-lucky gardens of the poor cottagers, where no elaborate schemes had been adopted and flowers had been left to grow for themselves in a happy tangle.

Many were the old-fashioned plants which he rescued from neglect, so that the rich man could once more enjoy the despised catmint, pinks, and humble flowers seldom to be seen except growing round the doorsteps of the poor.

With those pictures in his eyes he set to work to pull the theories of gardeners to pieces.

He was not afraid to make extremely rude remarks, nor to include many of England's stateliest homes in his list of what he calls pretentious places. " There was hardly a country seat," he wrote, " that was not marred by the idea of a garden as a conventional and patterned thing." Even the Royal Horticultural Society did not escape his castigation. Especially abhorrent to him were the " designs which may be quite all right on the surface of a carpet," but not on the surface of the much enduring earth. Yet he was no fanatic obsessed by a single idea, and nothing enraged him more than to be thus misunderstood. " They think I want to bring the wilderness in at the window," he wrote, " I who have given all my days to save the flower garden from the ridiculous ! " Where formality was indicated by the lie of the land, by the existence of walls or terraces, he was quite prepared to accept it. In his own garden he had a south terrace laid out with flagged paths and square beds, which was one of the prettiest bits of formality imaginable.

The real originality of Mr. Robinson's methods lay in his choice of what to grow and how to grow it. In his own square beds, for instance, where he grew principally roses, he also grew clematis, whose purple clusters rose above low shrubs of silvery grey, and furthermore he smothered the ground with pansies and even with low rock-plants, horrifying the rosarian whose conception of a rose-garden had been one of savagely pruned bushes of uniform height, with bare ground in between, liberally disfigured by mulches of unsightly and unsavoury manure. Then high up into his trees he flung great festoons of vine, honeysuckle, jasmine, and again roses ; in fact anything that would climb and cling, draping the upper branches with an unexpected beauty. Clematis he would grow not only on posts or pergolas in the accepted way, but would trail it along almost at ground level, so that the passer-by looked down into the upturned face of the starry flower. It was noticeable, however, that in all this riot of planting, nothing was ever allowed to become disorderly : he knew to perfection the art of concealing art. Everything was managed in such a way that each flower looked as though it had grown there of its own accord, and yet was displaying its colour, its shape, and its habit to the best advantage.

The efforts of these first daring rebels produced the gradual change which crept over gardening taste under the influence of their writings and their own example. Little by little one began to hear of such novelties as the woodland garden, the wild garden, the swamp garden, the orchard garden, and of separate enclosed gardens devoted to flowers of one colour or to the flowers of one season. Then began also the flood of new introductions from other countries ; China, Japan, Tibet contributed seeds and shrubs and flowering trees in ever-increasing quantities ; the United States and South America and Africa sent their share. A revival of the older roses also took place, so that in addition to the stunted and often scentless hybrid teas and perpetuals, people began again to plant the old moss and musk, the beautiful specie roses which fling up their long strands in wild profusion, the old damasks and Gallicas which had practically vanished from the gardens of the well-to-do.

Gardeners

GARDENS have behaved in an extraordinary way this year
(1938). Looking back upon my garden-diary, I find that on
January 26th the blue primroses were in full flower, thus preceding
their ordinary flowering period by about two months. Primroses,
even the blue ones, have no right to start flowering in profusion
until March or April. Then on March 9th I find a note saying
' all primroses flowering in earnest ', and towards the end of the
month another note to the effect that the garden appears to have
gone mad, and that the pink clematis montana is out in company
with tulips, hyacinths, anemones, and even a few of the flag irises.
By April 1st we were eating asparagus from the open ; by Easter
I was picking roses. But there is no need to go on with the tale.
Everyone knows that gardeners invariably say the season has been
exceptional, only this year it happens to be true.

I find gardeners disconcerting people. Either they know
infinitely more about the subject than I do, or else they know
infinitely less. Seldom do I encounter one with whom I can
discuss our common topic on equal terms. The gardener who
knows more is impossibly highbrow, and makes me feel as small
as a board-school child trying to discuss mediæval Latin literature
with, say, Miss Helen Waddell ; the gardener who knows less
makes me feel as though an earnest culture enthusiast said :
" Do tell me something about *The Shropshire Lad* ; it's a play,
I know, but I've never seen it." This, by analogy, is what happens
when somebody points to a delphinium and says : " How they have
improved lupins recently, haven't they ? " How should one
reply ? To correct the speaker sounds patronising ; to pass over
the slip in silence destroys the possibility of further comment.

National Parks

THE love of the English for natural beauty in all forms is, however, one of their most endearing characteristics. I was talking to a lady, a stranger, not so very young either, who had cheerfully travelled a hundred miles by bus on a hot day in order to visit a garden thrown open to the public. Looking out of the bus windows as they drove along the country roads, she told me, had not been the least part of her enjoyment. It made me wonder, as I had often wondered before, what the English landscape had been like a hundred years ago, before the builders and the bungalow-dwellers had started to ruin it. Parts of Surrey, for example, before it became suburbanised, must have been remarkably beautiful. The corollary to this reflection was to wonder still more what the English landscape would be like a hundred years hence, and the picture evoked was so appalling in its possibilities that I staggered, for the rapidity and efficiency with which building societies and their clients are doing their work of debasement all over the country can surely be equalled by no other branch of trade. As a character remarked in a Flers-et-Caillavet play : " Vous avez un flair, une sureté dans la gaffe—c'est du génie."

It was thus with some relief that I remembered that a campaign for the establishment of National Parks had been launched by Mr. Norman Birkett under the auspices of the Council for the Preservation of Rural England. One may hope that if this admirable scheme is pursued with all the vigour that well-advised and responsible enthusiasts can throw into it, something may yet be done before it is too late to safeguard areas of Great Britain for posterity. The scheme is ambitious, but not Utopian. If carried into effect, it would mean that such regions as the Marlborough Downs, stretches of sea-coast, the Norfolk Broads,

Dartmoor and Exmoor, the Peak and Dovedale, the Lake district, a large part of Wales, and most of the Highlands, including the Hebrides, would come under control and that the advance of vandalism might be stopped. Although the scheme would entail a certain expenditure of public money, I refuse to believe that our nature-loving public would grudge a few hundreds of thousands (not millions) to be expended for a benefit which it will very particularly appreciate.

The Kentish Landscape

AT the moment of writing these words, Kent is looking absurdly like itself. Cherry, plum, pear, and thorn whiten the orchards and the hedgerows ; lambs frolic ; the banks are full of violets and primroses ; the whole landscape displays itself as an epitome of everything fresh and innocent which has drawn ridicule upon the so-called school of Georgian poets. It is a simple delight which pleases everyone, from the unsophisticated to the sophisticated. Why affect to despise it ? Year after year I enjoy it more, and reflect with pride that my own county offers a fair presentment of the English scene to the foreigner travelling in his Pullman between Dover and London.

He, of course, cannot know it as we know it, though on his way up to London he is accorded a generous glimpse of the valleys of the Beult and the Medway. He sees the orchards and the hop-gardens ; orchards he has seen before in his own Normandy, but the hop-gardens strike him as very peculiar and individual, opening and shutting as they do while the train flashes past. If he does not already know what they are, he is reduced to asking an obliging stranger for the explanation. Those tall bare poles, that elaborately knotted string, those ploughed acres—what does it all mean ? The explanation is forthcoming : it is English beer. Of course : this is Kent. He looks out again with renewed interest, he remembers that this is called the garden of England.

Then his train slides into London, and he forgets about Kent.

But we, who live in Kent, do not forget about it and have no wish to do so. Intimately, not dramatically, it unfolds itself month by month. There are other landscapes more sensational, more romantic, more picturesque. This is a country-side which needs knowing. It needs a close and loving knowledge of the woods, the lanes, the villages, the changes of light, and the lost

113

places. It needs, perhaps, a spirit far removed from the speed
and competition of modern life to know and love it completely.
One must be satisfied with small and subtle things. One must
have time to absorb. Otherwise one is in very much the same
position as the man in the train, flashing through, registering
merely the passing comment : " Very pretty, yes, very pretty
indeed."

Living here, we realise more than the prettiness, the tenderness, the intimacy, we realise also the variety which can be ours
for a little trouble. I wonder what picture the word ' Kent '
evokes most readily in the minds of its lovers. For one of us,
it will be acres and acres of blossoming trees ; for another, the
short sunny slopes of the chalk hills ; for another, the wide
skies and lush meadows of Romney Marsh ; for another, the sea-
coasts ; for another, a bluebell wood and the sunlight falling
through the young green of the beeches. There are the slow
streams and the stone bridges, composing exquisitely with the
tower of the village church beyond. There are the villages
themselves, many as yet unravished—Yalding, Smarden, Chidding-
stone, Brenchley ; the little towns which preserve their charm
and dignity such as Tenterden with its wide main street and the
decency of its small Georgian houses, Cranbrook rocketing up
and down hill, crowned by the white windmill and its noble sails.
There are the dens and the hursts, with the miles of pleasant
country in between, and the pink cottages tucked into odd corners,
bright as a painter's palette with their jumble of flowers. All this
is Kent, and all indubitably English.

Sentimentally, we may linger over some of the lovely place-
names : Sutton Valence, Appledore, Stone-cum-Ebony, Capel-le-
Ferne, Damian in the Blean, and the three Boughtons, Aluph,
Malherbe, and Monchelsea. Historically our associations need
fear competition with no other county : four of the Cinque Ports
are ours, the Pilgrims' Way, and majestic Canterbury. We have
plenty of food for pride, either as men of Kent or Kentish men.

But how true, in actual fact, is this idyllic picture? We all know the optimistically misleading style of the average guide-book, in which we are conducted by the enthusiastic author from one enchanted spot to another, little paradises of rural retirement, as secluded as when Cobbett passed between our meadows on his famous Rides. Here is nothing, if the author is to be believed, to mar the prospect or rudely to jerk the dreaming mind. Every now and then, of course, the author gets confronted by some evidence of ugly utilitarian modernity to which he can blind neither himself nor his readers, and then in a fine indignation he lets himself go in several pages of lamentation, leaving us with the impression that these eyesores are of rare and strictly local occurrence, restricted to a few square miles or acres of victimised landscape, unlikely to impose themselves on a smaller scale on the happy wanderer who has the privilege of following his guidance down the by-ways. How far, I wonder, have I been guilty of giving the same misleading impression? One must be strict in these matters, even at the cost of some nasty truths.

Let me admit, then, that I have dwelt on the favoured corners and have left unmentioned those which one would rather pass with averted eyes. There is no denying that parts of Kent are dangerously near to London, and that the progressive spirit of the Southern Railway has brought them within a point of accessibility which can only be called suburban. The railway company, the road-makers, and the building societies have worked together in a morticed harmony which, applied to international problems, would soon produce a desirable settlement of world-affairs. The owners of the land, acting either under the stress of financial compulsion or allured by the temptation of a quick and certain profit, have lent their co-operation by large sales of property to enterprising speculators. On the part of all concerned there has been a general agreement to ' develop ' the residential possibilities of one of England's loveliest counties. The only pity is that under this process of development the county should so rapidly be ceasing to be lovely.

It is necessary, to-day, to know exactly where to go in order to find the unspoilt beauty where the true country-lover may rest his soul. My only plea in defence of my own veracity is that such retreats do still exist in Kent, more generously than the frequenter of main roads could possibly imagine.

We who care about such things view with alarm the spread of what we can only regard as damage. Daily, we see our fine trees being felled and their place taken by concrete posts slung with chains in front of shoddy buildings. Screaming red roofs and half-timber (no more solid than ply-wood) spring into being amongst our mellow cottages. Small wonder that we ask ourselves where it is going to stop, or, in a more practical spirit, what can possibly be done about it.

We do not wish to be reactionary or to deny the necessity of modern demands. Accommodation must be found, both for the working-man whose legitimate business keeps him to the district and for the daily-breaders and the week-enders whose desire is for a ' cottage in the country '. The natural consequences of these needs appear respectively in the form of council cottages and the small villa or bungalow. To the credit of the local councils it must be said that their productions are frequently of decent design, workmanlike construction, and æsthetically quite creditable. They could be better, of course, but they could also be a great deal worse. The same credit can scarcely be given to the large-scale contractors who supply the myriads of small ' homes ' so temptingly offered on easy terms, nor to those members of the public who snap them up so quickly that the advertisement board which was there yesterday will be gone by to-morrow. For this standardised trash I could wish only one fate : that it should all be miraculously transported and dumped as one large new city in the plumb Middle West of America.

Let me not be misunderstood. I recognise fully that ' develop-

ment ' must take place ; that sellers of land and contractors must make their profits ; that the new owner and occupier must be satisfied as to convenience and cheapness. But still I wonder whether the outcome of all these separate requirements need be of such unexceptionable hideousness ? I have heard it said that the whole trouble arises because there is no central control, and that the present haphazard system can produce only what it does actually produce ; I have even heard it suggested that an official committee of supervision for the whole country should be appointed under the auspices of the Office of Works. The men whom I privately heard making this suggestion were Lord Curzon and Mr. Ramsay MacDonald, two very different types of men, the patrician and the politician, yet both inspired by the same wish to preserve the beauty of their country. There is much to be said for such a scheme, but there are also a great many obvious objections to raise against it. In its favour it may be said that the taste and experience of an expert advisory board would in the aggregate be better and more valuable than the taste of the average builder and of the public for whom he caters ; against it may be said that in matters of taste few men with strong prejudices agree (and from such men the advisory board would presumably be drawn) and that one generation would almost certainly condemn the voice of the other. It is also evident that the indignation aroused by the restrictions necessarily imposed by such a board would be extreme, for our national character comprises a strong dislike of interference in our private affairs, and in a non-totalitarian state it is difficult to believe that a man would tolerate dictation in so private and personal a matter as the choice of his own home. If he likes bow-windows with stained glass, sham beams, or scarlet roofing, what authority can venture to forbid him to have it ? The only appeal is to his own discretion and sense of fitness ; but the sad truth is that the taste of the public is demonstrably bad. It prefers the ornate to the simple, the pretentious to the modest, and the consequence is that the small margin available in the estimate goes into something showy rather than into the honest domestic architecture whose survivals provide one of the minor beauties of our country. It seems only a foolishly Utopian dream to hope to raise the standard by even the most tactful methods of propaganda, yet the fact remains that a change of heart in the public alone would produce a change of method in the builder.

It appears to me that something might be done by organising

open competitions among the regional architects. As men familiar with the district they would have a good chance of understanding its needs, both practical and æsthetic : the treatment of brick, stone, plaster, tiles, or thatch, as the case might be, would come naturally to them as part of their daily life. The winning entries in these competitions should be displayed as a kind of bait to the public in several ways, either by photographs of the design in local papers, or exhibited in the post offices, or, best of all, as actual constructions to be let or sold. It is conceivable that with a *de facto* example before their eyes, some prospective purchasers might turn from the monstrosities to which at present they are offered no alternative, and where some led the way others might follow. There is no real reason why a presentable house or cottage should not be erected conveniently and inexpensively, nor should the solution unduly tax the ingenuity of the designer. His scope would indeed be varied and extensive, for apart from private dwellings the public requirements are great, and in the creation of new streets, new suburbs, even new villages, I can imagine a lively excitement to an inventive man. There is nothing necessarily to be said against the garden-city, of which indeed one has appreciated some attractive examples ; the garden-village, in the country, complete with church, school, shops, and even a central community garden as well as gardens to the individual houses, might invite the envy of strangers from miles around and cause us to forget the shudder usually aroused by the mere sight of the words ' building developments '. It should also be possible, by the extension of such schemes, to concentrate activities in more definite areas, instead of letting them straggle in their present happy-go-lucky fashion all over the place.

The isolated bungaloid effort, admittedly, is difficult to cope with, since you cannot prevent a man from buying a plot of ground where he likes and putting up whatever he likes on it. It seems very strange that a man who has the taste and sensibility to wish to live among beautiful surroundings should not also have the taste to see that his own abode is probably the one thing which ruins them ; but so it is. Here, again, the bait of a suitable, non-discordant sample might do more than many pages of written exhortation and entreaty. Many people, small blame to them, prefer the convenient modern dwelling to the picturesque but earwiggy old creeper-covered cottage where the alternative is either to crawl about bent double or else to bang your head on every lintel. There is no reason why they should not have it ; there is also no reason why they should make it impossible to look across miles of country where nothing breaks the eye's delight.

Plant-hunting

THERE are certain occupations which I enjoy enormously in theory, and do actually enjoy in practice provided I need pursue them only once or twice a year. One of these is plant-hunting. I am not, alas, referring to anything so adventurous as an expedition with yaks across Tibet, nor even to the more accessible delights of walking over Alpine meadows or Dolomitic screes where every yard is blown with the flowers that so signally refuse to flourish in one's own garden. I refer to the far milder and more modest ambition of discovering the rarer species of our native orchises for oneself in their own habitat.

The perseverance is great, and the reward may be small. One may have to creep, stooping, one's face lashed by brambles, one's hat torn from one's head, one's back breaking, through acres of hoary dogwood and Way-faring tree in search of the Military orchis which one never finds. Militarism being (one hopes) at the low ebb in this country, perhaps *Militaris* has gone into retreat.[1] One knows it should be there ; but either it has been picked by some marauder or eaten off by rabbits. So one has to content oneself with the ubiquitous tway-blade and its dingy green flower. *O. Militaris* has disappeared. One emerges at last from the dark inhospitable depths of the wood and finds oneself on the open down-land, where it is possible to breathe the air again and stretch the muscles. Here, surely, even at the cost of crawling over some hundreds of acres with eyes fixed to the ground, it might be possible to find a Green Man or even a fly or a spider ? The discovery of a Lizard is of course beyond all reasonable dreams ; but still, one never knows. One's luck might be in.

---

[1] *Written in June*, 1958.

Orchidaceæ

I WENT on such an expedition recently with two friends. We did not find much, it is true ; or, rather, we found none of the real rarities. That, however, never matters, for the compensations are so rich : the small, lost, down-land churches, miles from the villages they are supposed to serve ; the wide windy skies, the grassy slopes, the deep valleys with farm-buildings exquisitely composed into the group of barns, house, and oasts with steep brown roofs. I heard someone say the other day that when he saw or read about such things, nothing else seemed to matter, neither European complications, nor wars, nor threats of wars— they were all forgotten. I felt the same myself, when eventually we found the Bee orchis growing beside a partridge's nest.

We had sought all day, and had found nothing, except *Orchis pyramidalis* and the Fragrant orchis (*Gymnadenia Conopsea*) in such profusion as to become common and a bore. Just at the right moment we came upon the rarer Bee. With the perfect tact of the true artist, the Bee had placed herself beside this abandoned nest : the chicks had flown, the eggs were left, broken but tidily arranged within their scoop of grass, pale brown shells neatly opened to expose their pale blue lining, and above these the Bee orchis brooded in full flower like an insect preparing to descend on whatever honey she might find within the range of a few rich yards. Yet she never moved. She stood there, static, above the partridge's nest and the broken eggs on the open down, her dark lip hanging sulkily. She was small, and rather difficult to find among the grasses ; and so was the partridge's nest, so well concealed ; but finding them both thus in juxtaposition seemed a small triumph on a plane of beauty one would not readily forget.

Owls

WHILE on the same expedition we came across a young owl. It was sitting in the middle of the lane, and although the big, black car I was driving advanced towards it like Juggernaut it refused to move. Instead, it turned round to face the bonnet and to bridle in fury, too young to fly from danger, but not too young to be cross. It was very cross indeed, quite prepared to defy the death that so imminently threatened it. Sitting right back upon its haunches, it fluffed out its wings and spat defiance at us. Move it would not. It blocked the road. We had to stop the car ; get out ; and politely shoo the little indignant owl to a safer place.

I like owls. I admire their intransigent spirit. I have respected them deeply ever since I met a baby owl in a wood, when it fell over dead, apparently from sheer temper, because I dared to approach it. It defied me first, and then died. I have never forgotten the horror and shame I experienced when that soft fluffy thing (towards which I had nothing but the most humanitarian motives) fell dead from rage at my feet.

I like owls, partly because they hoot, and partly because they are so beautiful when they fly by night. Two white barn-owls live and breed in a barn where I live. Year after year, they have duly reared their brood. Year after year, I have seen them sail out across the fields seeking for provender, and have seen them return, ghostly, with things in their claws that I would prefer not to investigate.

I dislike owls for reasons that I had better leave to another note. Beautiful and poetic as owls are, they have other aspects which the realist cannot ignore. I shall therefore revert on a future occasion to their more unpleasant habits and to the contents of their stomachs.

Athene noctua

I WAS gratified to receive a letter from a reader saying that he could hardly wait for me to reveal the horrors that owls included in their nightly diet. He was under the impression, he said, that they lived principally on mice, bats, and beetles. Well, he was almost right ; and I fear that my revelations will interest him less qualitatively than quantitively. The variety of the victims is less impressive than the numbers in which they are consumed. When we consider that a pair of young barn owls kept under observation during the space of three weeks devoured one hundred and twenty shrews, forty-five rats, and sixty mice, varied only by a lark, a sparrow, and a partridge, we can estimate that their greed was not paralleled by their selectiveness. In other words, they ate anything they could get, and never seemed to tire of the monotony. An analysis of the pellets cast by adult barn owls gives a wider range, seven hundred pellets supplying the evidence for one thousand five hundred shrews, ninety voles, two hundred mice, nineteen sparrows, one greenfinch and two swifts. Another analysis, of a mere seventy-five pellets, gives the remains of sixty-nine shrews, twenty-nine voles, sixteen mice, thirty-seven birds, and a few dung beetles.

It would seem, then, that the owl is a valuable ally of the farmer, since it attacks chiefly the mischievous small enemies of the farm. The barn owl certainly is an ally, and anyone who destroys a barn owl is committing a foolish crime against his own interests. But what about the Little Owl, *Athene noctua* ? [After all, we ought, I suppose, to remember that the phrase ' Owls to Athens ' was once the equivalent of Coals to Newcastle.] Every now and then, in the Silly Season, the Little Owl becomes News. Is it useful, or mischievous ? Ought we to exterminate or encourage it ? No one has decided. Personally I think that the Little

125

Owl does more good than harm, since although it may destroy a few small birds during its hunting, it also destroys a number of pests such as rats and slugs. My view is, that the Little Owl ought to be spared. The more owls we have in this country, the better for both the poet and the farmer.

Owls Brood

I FIND something curiously touching in the quiet patience of a nesting bird. Day after day, at whatever hour one visits the nest, she is sitting there, close, warm, and lonely. One wonders what her thoughts may be ; what fears may assail at the approach of footsteps ; what deep instinct informs her of the final reward of her perseverance. The courage of some of these small creatures is indeed remarkable ; I have inadvertently put my hand right on to a thrush, and had my finger sharply pecked by a blue-tit in a drainpipe. Not so a Little Owl, nesting in a hollow apple-tree I pass every morning on my way to breakfast. Long before I have reached the tree she is out and away, flying off with the peculiarly noiseless flight which suggests twilight far more than the dews of summer morning. Once or twice I have deceived her ; crept up to her tree, and seen her cowering, head drawn back, ready to strike, a wicked eye looking up at me from the darkness. I was afraid she might desert her nest, a squalidly messy affair, but she shows no sign of doing so, and I look forward to the day when five recoiling babies will huddle at the bottom of the hollow trunk.

Cygnus olor

THE disagreeable though sociable cygnet which once insisted on sitting beside me while I weeded, was finally and firmly transferred to the lake where, after several attempts to return on foot to the garden, it at last consented to settle down, exchanging my company for that of the solitary, older swan. By that time it had changed its plumage from grey to white, and the two of them swam round together, gravely circling in full Jovian majesty. I was pleased by this, since the remarkable ungainliness of a swan waddling on land is equalled only by the beauty and dignity of a swan sailing on its proper element, and I had not enjoyed the spectacle of the cygnet making a fool of itself. They made a fine pair. The sex of the cygnet was, however, still undetermined ; anxiously I watched the colour and shape of its beak, whether it would turn from a buttercup yellow to orange, whether it would develop a big blob or a relatively small one. Much to my relief the beak continued to show every sign of femininity. The cygnet was obviously not a cob, but a pen. The older swan, for his part, grew more and more aggressively masculine. He became more and more possessive and protective. I began to think of them as he and she. The old gentleman whom I have mentioned elsewhere in these notes, the old gentleman who looks after Jacob's sheep and who has ideas of his own, still insisted that they were of the same sex. He was only slightly disconcerted when in May they started to make a nest. Two cobs, he maintained, often did that.

For a time I feared that his interpretation of the curious morality of swans might be correct. It was quite in vain that I walked round the lake murmuring :

'And she might be that sprightly girl who was trodden by a bird.'

My incantation seemed to take no practical effect at all. They made two nests in succession and abandoned them both. Then one day the ex-cygnet was observed to be sitting patiently, continuously, proudly, on the third attempt at a nest. By then I was sure.

The old gentleman was sure too, indeed there could be no denial ; but being a real countryman he was not prepared to retreat easily from his position. He announced to me that ' they ' had laid five eggs, thus denying by implication that either had been more responsible for the eggs than the other ; then added (rather inconsistently, I thought) that they owed their parenthood entirely to the fact that he had fed them with bread throughout the winter. I accepted both these theories without wasting time in argument.

Six weeks later the eggs hatched out. Most young birds are noticeably plain, their beaks being too large for their faces and their feathers too sparse for their bodies. The mouse, the rabbit, the puppy, the kitten, however delightful later on, are not attractive to even the most ardent animal-lover in their first, blind, naked stage. This drawback did not apply to the little cygnets. They were full of charm from the start ; moreover, they could swim at once, and thus fulfilled their function without delay. The little flotilla followed the mother in close formation, bobbing on the ripples, ducking their heads in search of food in absurd imitation of their parent. It was pretty to see her shelter them with her body when the wind blew too strong and manœuvre them between the rushes into quieter water. On the second morning I counted only four instead of five, and wondered where the fifth had gone. I could not believe that even a fox would have faced those great angry wings, but there was no doubt : only two pairs of grey fluff followed in the parental wake. Then a small grey head poked up through the mother's feathers, emerging on a thin neck curved into a mark of interrogation, out of what must surely be the snowiest, softest place of refuge in the world.

Podiceps ruficollis

READING about the manners of birds described by other people is agreeable enough, but the interest is impersonal and savours too much of a transient curiosity over odd habits, much as we might experience in reading about the Trobrianders. The Trobrianders are unlikely to affect, or even to enter, our lives. Nor is the Great Auk, or the Chiloe Wigeon, but the moment a personal discovery, however humble, comes our way, how very different is our response. The excitement of discerning the nest of a long-tailed tit among some exceedingly thorny rose-bushes is enough to make us feel that we are really in touch with the queer hidden world of nature. We knew of course theoretically that long-tailed tits did construct such remarkable homes to rear their brood, but never until we saw it with our own eyes did we quite believe it.

It was thus with pleasure and surprise that, scrambling round the lake, I observed a strange dank patch of mud on the extreme tip of a fallen willow bat, half in and half out of the water, and knew it for the nest of a Little Grebe. The surprise was unwarranted, for the Little Grebe commonly frequents our lakes and ponds, and there was nothing at all noteworthy in the fact that it had thus chosen to honour my own small piece of water. Still, there it was, and I was pleased. More, I felt even proud. ' The Little Grebe ', I murmured to myself, snobbishly avoiding the more popular name of dabchick. ' *Podiceps ruficollis ruficollis* ', I might have added, but owing only to my ignorance I didn't.

Instead, I approached cautiously to the very verge of the lake. The nest was right out in the water, balanced on its horizontal bat, the tiny waves washing up to it as the breeze blew. Thanks to the ingenuity of the builder, no one would ever have taken it for a nest at all. It was very different from the neat, dry nests

of the neighbouring moorhens, carefully plaited with papery reeds, like cheap waste-paper baskets, among the stumps of old trees out of reach of water or foxes. The nest of the Little Grebe was, in comparison, a messy affair that made one wonder why two kinds of water-bird, living in such close proximity and in precisely the same circumstances, should have evolved so different a method of dealing with the same dangers and the same difficulties.

Sitting down to watch for anything that might happen, I reflected how greatly I should dislike to start my life from such a home. One instinctively thinks of a nest as a warm, cosy thing—the incubator system foreseen by nature. This nest bore no relation to the incubator system whatsoever. It was muddy, it was wet. It looked cold and sodden. It was, in fact, nothing but a dab of wet mud. A strand of wild honeysuckle grew unhappily out of it. No eggs were visible because the Little Grebe has the ingenious idea of covering her eggs with wet leaves whenever she absents herself from her responsibilities. Frighten her, and off she goes, after hiding her treasure. This was evidently what had happened, but after I had been sitting there for a few minutes there came a rustle among the reeds and a neat head peeped out, sensed my presence, and again disappeared. I scarcely liked to remain on the watch, because it so obviously distressed the bird whom I could now see sailing round on the outskirts, worried and anxious. The nest might be messy, but it was the only thing she knew how to do, and it was dear to her. Happy though I was, sitting among the spent bluebells and the ragged robins on a summer afternoon, I got up and went away, not to distress the Little Grebe unduly.

A few weeks later a quick scuffle on the bank drew my attention to a second nest, even wetter, messier, and more dabby than the first. It was not even perched on a bat, but floated independently with no visible support. I rowed out to it, since it could be reached only by boat, stirred the dank leaves, and found the warm eggs lying beneath. The sudden warmth of the eggs startled me, coming after the coolth of the water and the soggy moisture of the nest. The warmth of the eggs and the coldness of the water seemed in significant contradiction : the warmth of life, the cold of Ophelia's death. The touch of those five warm eggs was one of those small, dulcet, delicately sensual experiences which one does not forget.

I know, however, that when presently I revisit those nests, the broods will be out swimming with their mothers, and at the first alarm will clamber on to their backs and be carried off into safety. It is one of the prettiest sights of the waterside, this soft scramble of chicks into the comfort of their mother's feathers.

Circus

DURING the summer months you may meet them on the country roads, a long file of caravans drawn by a traction engine. Rocking and swaying, they crawl elephantine between the hedges, gaudily painted ; the merry-go-round and the swing-boats, the animals' cages and the tent-poles, the ponies following on a rope. These are the humble village circuses that pitch their brief camp in a field, beat their drums, blow their trumpets, put out their streamers, pocket their gate-money, and depart again after a prodigious litter and ruin of demolition and repacking. These are the humble circuses of summer ; where they hibernate I do not pretend to know. They come with the swallows and leave us with the autumn, a ragged, bright, thievish, vagrant fraternity, associated with sun and dust and parched fields ; they are the brood of summer, and for them winter has no place.

But in the winter their grander brethren blossom out in the glare of great towns. The Christmas holidays bring them, and with them their paraphernalia of wonders that are always fundamentally the same, and always just sufficiently different. What painter could sit unmoved at a circus-ring, his fingers not twitching to hold the brush ? The lights are there, flaring and crude ; the shadows, cavernous and brutal ; the shapes are there, in the pale ring of the arena and in the shining, twirling figures, whether sheathed in silver and purple, or blotched with paint in the eternal clumsiness of a clown. Hoops and horses, velvet ropes and glittering trapeze. Violent light from reflectors overhead, and the dim tiers of the audience, now transfixed and agape, now released into a sudden riot of stirring and applause.

The arena lures us, as it lured the Romans to the Coliseum, as it lures the Spaniards to the bull-ring. It is a little epitome of life itself, where, concentrated under the rays of the limelight, men

come safely through situations of skill and danger. It seems astonishing that they *should* come through, but somehow they always do. And that, I think, is the weak spot of the circus. Not that we secretly desire an accident—though some psychologists would make us believe that under every expression of goodwill lies a subconscious and diabolical intent—but that we are persuaded, from the start, that juggler and acrobat are fully able to perform successfully the feats they set out to perform. Be it never so seemingly impossible, we know, coldly sophisticated as we are, that the man has not undertaken a job beyond his strength.

Therefore, we scarcely want to see him execute it. We are convinced, even before he has embarked upon his enterprise. The
moment we arrive at the circus we turn into born believers. We
accept the fact that the man can ride a bicycle along a tight-rope
in mid-air ; that he can pause mid-way (though heaven knows
that we ourselves cannot remain motionless upon a bicycle on firm
ground, let alone upon a tight-rope), and that he can without loss of
equilibrium put up a parasol and again without loss of equilibrium
allow a little boy to climb upon his shoulders. But in spite of our
confidence, in spite of the fearful thrill at our hearts, we are
humanely cowardly somewhere for the safety of a fellow-mortal—
we would rather not see him do it. He can do it all right, of
course, but just suppose . . .

The worst of it is that children, for whom the circus is primarily
designed, are as trusting as their elders. Perhaps they miss half
the thrill, being without that whisper of uneasiness, that terror
that something might, after all, go wrong. They are not torn, as
we grown-ups are torn, between the rather bored conviction that
the man can do it, and the qualm that perhaps, after all, he can't.
The man to them is a grown-up, and consequently omnipotent.
That he can keep twelve plates in the air, or ride a bicycle along a
tight-rope, is no more marvellous than that their father should
be able to blow smoke down his nose. Danger, in itself, means
nothing to them. ' Take care, you'll hurt yourself ', that daily
and familiar formula, means, at most, the possibility of a grazed
knee. They cannot envisage the mess and ruin of a human
frame. And so, with open mouth and upturned nose, they
serenely, politely, follow the fabulous feats enacted for their
benefit.

They like the clowns, on the whole preferring to see a man
funny than imperilled. Their applause of the clowns is spon-
taneous, not perfunctory. The clown knows the value of a
pretended failure ; he knows that to stumble over the first attempt
will bring a more sympathetic and rapturous appreciation of his

ultimate success.   He has brought himself down to the human and fallible level ; he has shown himself to be no Omnipotent ; he has come closer to the understanding of a child.

What a world, to be sure !   One would like to know something of the mentality behind the scenes.   Do they take their gyrations quite for granted, or does it give a new outlook upon life to behold an audience twice daily upside-down ?   Is there any real satisfaction in being a contortionist ?   The most disheartening part of these accomplishments must be, surely, that they are of no use outside a circus.   Very rarely, in ordinary life, is one called upon to pick up a handkerchief with one's teeth from the back of a galloping horse.   It must be depressing in the extreme to have to spend so many hours in the practice of such unpractical achievements.   They are not really an equipment, even when mastered. They are only a livelihood.   I doubt even whether the lady who leaps so lightly upon the rounded rump of the piebald horse would cut much of a figure in the hunting-field ; I have a suspicion that she would come off at the first fence.   And the tight-rope cyclist might well be tumbled off his saddle on a greasy road.   It is sad, but perhaps at the same time comfortable to our vanity, to reflect that the infallible and indestructible gods of the arena may be, in ordinary life, rather less competent than ourselves.

Between two Seasons

SUMMER is still here officially, but subtle hints have already been thrown out by its successor among the seasons. There comes a morning, always, at this time of year when one awakes to the realisation that one's knees and the tip of one's nose are unexpectedly cold, and, still drowsy, scrabbles to regain the blankets one had flung off during the earlier part of the night ; then, aroused to full consciousness, leaps from bed to gaze out of the window. What has happened ? The familiar summer aspect has changed. A faint white mist hangs between the trees, a chill dampness soaks the hollyhocks. A few pallid sunbeams struggle through the mist. There is dew upon the grass, and diamond spider-webs along the hedges. For the first time one notices that the apples out in the orchard are beginning to redden.

A couple of hours later all this is forgotten, and summer

reigns again as though her sway had never been threatened.
The sunbeams have won the victory over the insidious white
mist, and in the hot, broad day the grass is again warm to the
touch, the hedges dry enough to rustle under the weight of a
bird. The adders have come out to sun themselves upon the stone.
The long mauve tassels of the buddleias are smothered with
butterflies and bees. From a distance comes the whirr of a reaper,
most summery of sounds, as the noble wheat falls sadly and
gracefully in widening bands. The brief ghostly apparition of
autumn has gone, but we know that any morning now it may be
renewed.

Eels

ON summer evenings it is pleasant to sit by the lake, watching the electric-blue dragon-flies quivering over the rushes while the sun declines and the big trout leap a foot out of the water. The stillness is broken by their splash and by the distressful cry of the moorhens, but these natural sounds leave the other inhabitants of the waterside untroubled. If you keep very still, the confidence which your arrival faintly disturbed will soon be re-established and a vole will scramble from the water almost at your feet. It gives a peculiar sense of intimacy with nature to realise that your presence is accepted without fear by the small and vulnerable creatures of bank and wood and to watch them going unalarmed about their normal business.

On such evenings, earlier in the year, you might almost hope to see an elver making its way over the damp grass from the ocean to the lake, a sight, it is said (I do not know with what truth), that no man has ever been privileged to witness. Eels, as everyone knows, are creatures of curious habits ; the Bermudas are not remote to them, and you may take it that the sinuous creature of our native ponds is probably better-travelled than many humans. It must be very tiring to be so constituted that one has to swim several thousands of miles in order to find sufficient depth of water in which to arrive at sexual maturity. A hundred fathoms of pressure is, I believe, the minimum necessary. But why the resulting elvers should then return to the haunts from which their parents had come, or should themselves obey the urge to seek the depths of the Caribbean in the fullness of time, is a mystery which none can answer.

All we know is that the little eels arrive, small and diaphanous, and are well-advised to avoid the cities of Bath and Bristol, where they traditionally run the risk of being made into elver-cakes. The

141

town of Melun is no place for them either, for Rabelais asserts that the eels of Melun screamed before being skinned alive. The eel, in fact, does not seem to meet with much human sympathy ; even the common sayings about him are disobliging. I wish, however, that we used his adjective more generally : ' An eely man ' seems to me an excellently descriptive expression.

Eels in Italy

SITTING by the Lake of Garda one evening after dinner, I observed a fishing boat about to leave the small harbour, and hailing the men I asked whether I might accompany them. A lantern hung at the prow, and under a great dim sail we very slowly drifted away from the shore. It was already dark ; the vague shapes of men bent over their gear, silently setting things in order. A figure squatting in the prow motioned to me to come beside him ; I saw then that he held a pronged spear-like weapon in his hand, and that between his knees crouched a little boy, ready and eager to unhook the lantern. At a signal he swung it overboard, and we peered down into the clear green depths of the water. It may have been deceptive, but I should have said we looked down through at least twenty feet of water so pellucid that the pebbles lying on the bottom were plainly visible. Not pebbles only, but droves of fish that darted by, and, under the fish, long coiling shapes that seemed almost somnolent compared with those quick-moving midgets. The man with the spear poised his weapon ; the little boy with the lantern cautiously lowered it until the light almost touched the surface. The coiling shapes writhed uneasily, and as they writhed, separating slightly from one another, the man with the spear struck. He struck with a gesture of singular beauty and precision, a gesture which in the fraction of a minute suggested all the centuries during which men, similarly armed, had struck down into those very waters. The dripping spear came up triumphantly, the snake-like victim impaled upon its prongs ; the little boy, excited but businesslike, sprang to disengage it from the barb. It was flung into the well of the boat, but the spearman had already lost interest and, with his dark little acolyte again lowering the lantern, was once more gazing down into the glaucous transparency.

The Hop-picking Season

THE hoppers are arriving in Kent. It is curious to observe that the moment the East-ender leaves his slum in Bermondsey or Rotherhithe for this annual expedition, he starts to cut quite a different figure in the public mind, ceases to be a mere and rather vulgar Cockney, and is instantly invested with all the attributes of romance. For three weeks in his drab year he is allowed to rank in picturesqueness with the gipsy. Why this should be so is a little difficult to explain. He dresses in the same way as he does in London, yet there is a difference between the Cockney and the hopper ; perhaps the red handkerchief knotted round the throat looks better in a field than in the slum. The tawdry muslins of his women make a bright and oddly foreign effect among the bines. The presence of many children turns the serious business of picking into something like a pagan festival, reminding me of the Neopolitan celebration when the local little boys spray their naked sunburnt bodies with the copper-sulphate used for the prevention of Phylloxera and prance about stained in turquoise blue between the olives and the vines at dawn, a scene which Leonardo might have found it in his taste to record in paint. The Londoners' children are neither so gay nor so pagan, but still a certain light-heartedness descends on all. It is very un-English in spite of being so essentially English. The hop-garden is a fair substitute for the vineyard, with its swags of green bunches so like the white muscat, its long leafy tunnels dappled with light, its brown canvas troughs filled with the pale flowers. Colour and gaiety reign in a way they never do at the other great country events such as hay-making or harvest.

This gaiety is reflected also in the trouble that the Cockney family takes to make its temporary home as lively as possible. The sleeping quarters provided are usually no better than a range of wooden huts—sometimes even an old railway coach—lime-washed inside, and supplied with a wooden bench and a couple of trusses of straw for bedding. Nothing more. It is all very clean, bare, and hard. Little can be said for it save that it is clean and (one hopes) weather-proof. Fortunately the families who have descended yearly upon the same hop-garden for several generations, grandmother, mother, and child, know exactly what to bring with them in order to turn the hut into a home. They bring coloured lithographs and lace curtains ; bedspreads and china ornaments, and by the time they have set out their treasures their little hovel looks as attractive as a Dutch interior. Then when the working day is over they gather round bonfires and rouse the quiet night with songs and piano-accordions.

In damp sunless weather the picture is different. We remember then that perhaps thanks to our climate we are a glum race. A peddler comes round crying mackerel at five a shilling ; alive they were, and swimming, this morning at sunrise, for the sea is not so very far away, but now the dead protruding eyes of fish stare at the pickers over the edge of the basket ; this has to do duty for song and sunburnt mirth. The pickers then contribute nothing of jollity. Sordid, pasty bundles, sitting on camp stools or wooden boxes, their muslins hidden away beneath their mackintoshes, their babies uncomfortably asleep in go-carts beside them, they strip the bines in gloomy silence, preoccupied solely with the completion of their tally. A tally to a family ; a big thing to fill, and only 1s. 5d. when you have done it. No wonder they are sometimes gloomy, especially when it rains. The grape is a fruit, the hop only a flower ; perhaps that makes all the difference.

It appears also that they do not wholly like being in the country. So long as the weather is fine they make the best of it, regarding it as a holiday to be enjoyed, almost an obligation, but then as day dies a certain alarm disquiets their souls. Away from traffic and street lights, they are frightened. The silence and the darkness of the fields perplexes them. They will not go about after dusk except in little bands. Toughs though they may be at home, they are not tough enough to stand the desolation of the darkened country-side. On the whole they feel rather relieved when the moment comes for them to climb into their charabancs or cars again and return to a mode of life they understand.

Perhaps, however, they will not much longer be called upon to add their picturesque touch to the country year. The bines, it is said, will soon be stripped by machinery. Oh, brave new world !

The Garden and the Oast

IT is the annual outing of the East End, but the East End cannot be expected to take any affectionate interest in our peculiarly local crops. These acres, representing several thousands of pounds, tended all the year by expert, almost instinctive, country hands, from the first training of the bine to the last fingering of the swollen flower, are turned over in the height of their fulfilment to the unskilled, unsympathetic mercies of the Cockney. Consider for a moment the care and vigilance which throughout the months of winter, spring, and summer have brought the gardens to their autumn state of fecundity. First, after the harvesting, the old bines must be cleared away ; then the pruning-knife must sever and select ; then, with the shooting of the new bine, up go the strings—strings reckoned by the ton ; six hundred miles of string, fixed to the ground at the bottom by women and boys, and to the permanent wires overhead by men on stilts, giant figures stalking between the poles in the bleak spring day. The bine begins to grow ; heavily fed, it will grow as much as two feet in a night, twining round the strings from right to left, for the hop cannot be persuaded to grow widdershins. You may think that a plant with so much energy might now be left for a little to its own devices. Make no such mistake. It has its enemies : mould and insects ; it has its remedies : wash and powder ; the enemy must be looked for, and the remedy applied unsparingly, even though the men with knapsacks blow hundreds of pounds sterling in fine sulphur dust into the air. The wind, too—a proper gale will do grand damage in the hop-garden. But the garden survives these dangers, and towards the end of August you are rewarded by the pale, imponderable clusters, well grown out, as you walk down the green, lovely aisles or mount your fixed ladders for a final inspection. It is then, when your expert judgment decides

147

that the flower is ripe for picking, that London lets loose its hordes and the garden is profaned by the presence of these philistines, and the fish-peddler cries his mackerel at five a shilling.

The profanation, however, marks but a brief stage in the history of the hop from bine to bottle. At the sole moment of its picking is the hop subjected to the hands that neither love, hate, nor understand it. Once picked into the pokes, when the garden begins to assume a dirty, dejected air, with the cut bines withering in their fallen heaps, the poles sticking up gaunt and useless, the wires overhead fluffy with the fringe of cut strings —once picked, the flower is hurried to the oasts, where skilled driers receive it. These are men who have been for thirty, forty, fifty years at their job. They handle their material and their implements as though they knew what they were about. Indeed, they disregard some of their implements, with a sort of contempt, such as the thermometer and the weighing-machine, referring to them only as a concession to convention, to corroborate their human judgment, or to satisfy the overseer, when their instinct is rarely proved at fault. This is pleasing, and as it should be. The hop is once more in hands that have the mastery over it.

All day the chimneys of the kilns have been smoking blue, but the life of the kiln does not slacken with dusk, when the pickers go home to their camp ; all night the process of drying goes on, to keep pace with the supply that has been pouring in from the garden. Inside the oast, we choke and cough with the sulphur ; the doors of the furnaces stand open for a fresh stoking, like the entrails of a ship, the pan of sulphur blue in the midst of the fire ; the men, demoniacal figures redly lit, shovel on the coal, slam the doors, throw down their shovels with horrible clang ; this ground-level of the oast is a place of violence. Propped against the wall, too, are brutal shapes, sacks as big as bullocks, with the white horse of Kent prancing painted across them, and their corners tied into ears like the ears of killed beasts.

But on the upper story the hop reassumes its character of pale

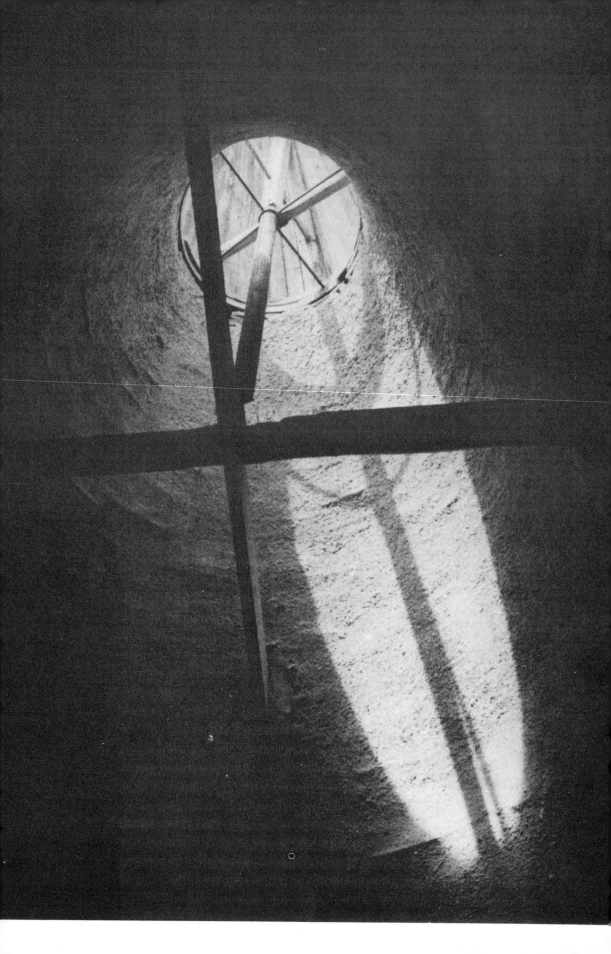

colour and feather weight. In the long, low, raftered loft, where
everything is whitewashed, the lanterns swing from the beams
above mountains of dried flowers on the floor, billowing heaps
of a ghostly pallor, an exquisite imponderability. Impossible to
give a name to their colour. It is a cross between ash and gold ;
the colour of dust-motes, of corn in moonlight, of fair hair under
a lamp. All the green has been taken from them in the drying ;
they are crisp and airy ; everything you touch is sticky with resin,
even the bristles of the brooms are knobby with resin gathered in
sweeping up the floor ; the pungent smell is in the air. The
lanterns throw the shadows of the rafters in sharp designs on roof
and floor. The men, dressed in white overalls, pile the heaps
higher with rake and scupper—huge scoops made of white canvas.
In one corner, where a hole gapes in the boards, two men shovel
the hops down the hole into the mouth of the sack which hangs
below, out of sight ; a great wheel spins round, the shadow of its
spokes whirling over the whitewashed wall, and the weight descends
into the sack, pressing, packing, till the flowers are squeezed into
solidity, and one believes at last what had always seemed so uncon-
vincing, that a ton of feathers weighs as much as a ton of lead.

This is all activity ; but the hops at their drying are quiet
and private. Doors along one side of the loft open on to the
upper chambers of the kilns, white, circular, the roof rising to a
point. The hops are spread knee-deep upon the floor. They are
green still, and a faint blue smoke rises through them. It is very
quiet in there, with a quality of solitude and vigil ; very warm
too, and heavily scented, inside the circular oast. The drier steps
into the sea of hops, and slouches through them, kicking them up.
Especially on the outside edges is it necessary to see that they shall
be evenly dried ; so he slouches round the wall, an old man in
white corduroys, travelling against the white wall, stealthily as it
seems, kicking up the pale green sea that faintly rustles, disturb-
ing the smoke into little wreaths and eddies. There is a medieval
flavour about it : the round chamber, the roof pointed like a

witch's hat, the white and green, the warmth, the smoke, the ancient man, the smell that creeps so soporifically over the senses.

Out in the yard, as you come away, the shafts of the waggons stick up at the stars, and the cowled chimneys point in a blacker darkness at the darkness of the sky. To the left lies the ruined garden, with aisles of bare poles waiting for next year's bine. You stumble down the lane, and at the corner turn to throw a glance at the group of kilns. A light appears in a little window, high up. You know then that the old drier has taken his lantern into the oast, and is slouching the hops, round and round the wall, in that furtive way, a mysterious rite, while in the loft the weight sinks rhythmically into the filling sack, and the overseer scribbles another ton upon his slate. There is no sleep for the men, and to-morrow the carts will come creaking up the lane with new loads from the gardens.

Humulus Lupulus

THE history of the hop is not uninteresting. Guinness is good for you ; but in the reign of Henry VI popular opinion took a different view, and the hop was condemned as ' a wicked weed '. By the time of Henry VIII the wicked weed had attained quite another status, having been officially introduced from Flanders for cultivation in Kent and two or three other counties. Even so, Henry VIII ruled that the brewer should not put any hops into the ale, since this addition would ' dry up the body and increase melancholy '. This ruling of an autocratic King did not prevent an irreverent subject of the Crown from writing, perhaps rather inaccurately,

> Hops, Reformation, Bays, and Beer
> Came into England all in one year.

The overwhelming proportion of those hops which came into England, never to depart, is grown in Kent, and has had its effect upon the landscape of the county in those characteristic pointed oast-houses, with their white vanes swinging to the wind. Most people must be strangely incurious. Nearly everybody must surely have seen oasts dozens of time, if only from the window of a train, yet if one lives near a group of them one is constantly asked what ' those odd-looking buildings ' are for. During the first weeks of September, anyone can see for himself what they are for. He can climb up into the upper loft and glance into the round turret where the deep green carpet of cones is spread drying in the hot fumes. He can watch the men shovelling the dried heaps through a hole in the floor, packing them tightly into the great sacks called pockets in which they are to be driven away to the brewer—the last stage in the endlessly complicated process of the hop-grower's year.

Harvest

'THE corn was orient and immortal wheat, which never should be reaped, nor was ever sown.' The harvest was long delayed this year, and it seemed indeed that the great corn-field would never be ready for the reaping. Day after day it continued green, lacking the Midas touch of the sun ; Lammas came and went without effect, yet the proverb records that after the Loaf-mass corn ripens as much by night as by day. The change came as imperceptibly as the growth of a child, until one morning I woke to the realisation that it was no longer green but yellow. Regretfully, I knew that the hour was approaching when the beautiful moving sea would go down before the sails of the reaper and nothing but the stubble remain until the plough should follow to turn it once more into furrows. Still the ripening loitered on the way. The pale yellow persisted without giving sign of deepening into the brown so prophetic of the crusted loaf. Evening after evening I went to look at the corn, half hoping, half fearing to observe the second change which would mean that harvest was at hand. There are two times of day when, for sheer beauty, it is most advisable to look at a cornfield : the early morning, when the shadows are long from the east, and the evening when the shadows are long from the west. Noon is too high overhead and less becoming. Of the two extremes, sunrise or sunset, sunset is greatly to be preferred, for then a sultry marriage takes place between the low deep light and the voluptuous field ; sunrise, beautiful though its shadows are, is really too young, fresh, and romantical. There is an age and an agelessness in corn which better suits the dying day.

Much can be said for moonlight also, though there would appear to be a contradiction between the dead blanching of the moon and the warm living of the corn. Yet they mysteriously marry. There have been evenings of late when the moon riding between Mars and Jupiter has lit the cornfield in a way that suggested the spiritual life alternating with the material life symbolised by the sun, both necessary to the bread by which man cannot live alone.

The corn is cut now, and the harvest in. The men worked till daylight failed them, cutting, carting, stacking, for the weather might spoil and other things more serious than the weather might spoil also. It was more than ever urgent to get the harvest in. In the few fields which are not yet carted the sheaves remain pitched upright, throwing cones of shadow like the black cones employed by map-makers as symbols to mark the site of Roman villas in Britain. Lammas came, Lammas went ; the Romans came, the Romans went ; the sheaves remain, the sheaves will go, they will be carted into the big barn and the field will be stripped empty until next year when other sheaves will stand in their place like dunces' caps marking the site of villas or tiny pyramids recalling the monstrous accomplishments of Egypt.

The corn was orient and immortal wheat . . .

Cornucopia

SUMMER goes down in a last splendid burst of lavishness. Even this year of 1938, about which so many complaints were heard, I could have gathered enough natural food within half an hour to keep several people from starvation for several days. The William pears need little more than a night in a dark cupboard before they turn sweet and yellow. The hedgerows are already hung with the black and red clusters of shining blackberries, and the nuts in their pale green sheaths are more abundant than I have seen them for many years. The fallen maggoty ones crack underfoot, as we tread reaching up to pull down the sound ones hanging overhead. The little white umbrellas of the mushrooms are dotted all over the fields. On the garden walls the peaches are no less rosy than the bricks, and the figs have turned as brown as a piece of old velvet. Out in the orchard, standing just high enough to have escaped the May frosts that ruined the blossom in the valleys, big green cooking apples drop with a thud into the grass among the violet cups of the autumn crocus.

Peace and plenty, if only for the moment.

Waste ?

I FIND that people vary considerably in their attitude towards the fruits of the earth. Some, true country-dwellers, put them to jealous use, and a well-stocked store-room is the result. There are few sights more agreeable than shelves neatly loaded with glass jars as coloured as jewels with jam, juice, and jellies ; the ruby of raspberry, the aquamarine of gooseberry, the fire-opal of marmalade, the pearls of white currant. Then there are—or should be—the big brown crocks full of chutney and of beans layered in salt ; the pails of eggs preserved in isinglass. There should also be large marrows laid aside ; and perhaps one of them may be hanging up, disembowelled and stuffed with brown sugar, destined eventually to produce a decoction of which it is said that one drink is quite enough and two a great deal too much. Add a few dangling bunches of dried herbs, and the store-room begins to wear the aspect it ought to wear. An air of proper pride presides over it ; a quiet, independent air ; a practical expression of trouble taken.

To-day few are left to take such trouble. Why layer beans in salt when a tin of peas can be bought for $8\frac{1}{2}d$. ? Why bother about blackberries when canned peaches arrive miraculously and cheaply from California and the Cape ? Why bother to cut the down out of bulrushes when Kapok cushions can be bought for a few pence ? So, gradually, the traditions are dying out even amongst the country people.

From the town-dweller one expects, and gets, a different point of view. It horrifies the town-dweller to observe the wastage that goes on. To him, unaccustomed to the lavishness of nature in potential foodstuffs, the free feast offered suggests nothing but perplexity and envy. " How can you leave all those good apples lying there ? " he says in righteous surprise.

158

" How can you allow half your vegetables to run to seed ? Why don't you send them to a hospital if you don't want them yourself ? You don't realise what they cost to buy in a shop."

The townsman is right, and yet wrong. Right, because it is true that sufficient advantage is nowadays not taken of many things which we could have for nothing (nothing, that is, but our own labour). Wrong, because in his ignorance he frequently does not know the reason. He does not realise that the windfalls are bruised and thus not worth the gathering except for jam. He has never been accustomed to let a proportion of his vegetables run to seed so that he may harvest it—another free gift—for next year's crop. There are many explanations the countryman could give him.

One thing, however, always does surprise me, and that is the indifference with which the hop-pickers regard the mushroom. I had always believed that mushrooms were considered a delicacy when you could not just wander out and collect them in the fields but had to buy them from the greengrocer ; I discovered, on the contrary, that the invasion of Londoners did not even recognise them for what they were but amused themselves by kicking them over with the toe of their boot while walking along. There they lay, broken and scattered, the lovely pink undersides like fishes' gills, turned black and sodden. I suppose that, growing the right way up in the field, they looked very different from the tumbled sooty heap in the greengrocer's basket. I pointed out the lost opportunity to a party of pickers from Bethnal Green. " What ! them mushrooms ? " they said incredulously. " Why, we thought they was toadstools."

Departure

THE pickers have nearly finished their job and will be leaving us at the end of this week. No longer shall we see the red light of their fires burning in the distance, nor, on a Saturday night, shall I be able to walk down to their huts, sit with them round the brushwood fire, and listen to their jokes and their songs. It is a scene which, with a difference, always carries me back to a ranch in California, where under the shelter of a great rock the cowboys would light their bonfire and sit round chanting endless sagas of the trail. There is no great rock here, and the stars are less enormous, but even in the tameness of my own familiar fields the sole illumination of the flames casts a wild beauty over the rough faces and the coloured scarves. The doors of the huts stand open, a little oil-lamp revealing each miniature interior ; the head of a sleepy child droops suddenly ; an armful of fresh brushwood makes the embers flare ; the plaintive notes of the accordion continue to rise and fall. It is nearly two o'clock in the morning ; the jokes, the dancing, and the ribald songs have ceased ; they have stopped dancing the Lambeth Walk ; the songs are all sentimental now—eternal Sehnsucht and eternal pain.

I shall miss the hoppers.

Controversial Topics

THAT last week of September 1938, excruciating though it proved at every moment to our strained nerves, enjoyed a singular outward beauty. September went down in a slanting golden sun, touching our familiar landscapes with a light so rich and mellow as to preclude all suggestion of irony. It seemed, indeed, inconceivable that devastation should fall suddenly on such a scene. Looking across at the harmless sunlit hills, the mind rejected the conception of violence. Men might be digging trenches in their gardens, and reason encouraged them to do so ; but still some deep old stupid optimism lurked, telling them that this was only a precautionary measure, not really (not in the last resort) necessary. They joked as they dug, and it was hard to tell whether their joking or their digging was the more sincere.

We dug a trench in the orchard here—a most inadequate trench which would certainly have fallen in at the first heavy rain, a most unscientifically constructed trench, which expressed the instinct to burrow into the friendly earth rather than any calculated attempt to provide a four or five years strong shelter against the attack of an efficient foe. Not that, out in the country as we are, danger seemed very likely ; but one never knows, thinking of Spanish villages and the swoop of machine-guns. So one must make provision. This sudden hasty burrowing into the earth struck one as truly horribly uncivilised : man seeking refuge from man under the peacefully ripening apples and pears of September—man turning himself into a frightened furtive threatened creature like a rabbit or a mole. Human dignity fell crashing from its unique state : it dug, it tunnelled, it hid itself away in the last desperate attempt to protect its vulnerable body. Shocking, and yet necessary. How wrong and foolish that such a necessity should arise between man and man. What would a visitor from another world, a more co-operative world, have felt about my rough trench dug hastily in the orchard ? Mars approaches, only thirty-six million miles away instead of forty-five, accompanied by two small moons, smaller than ours, more rapid in their flight ; and we beneath the red planet cower between walls of yellow clay. There are indeed times when absurdity can appear more tragic than high tragedy ; and so I thought when, visiting a rich man's garden, I came upon an elaborately revetted dug-out concealed among the rhododendrons.

I suppose that the psychological effect of that week acted upon all of us differently. None of us could have predicted what associations of thought it would set up in our minds, as a reaction after the immediate danger had passed temporarily away. There was the man who remarked that he wished he was living again in 1916, because then he knew that the war would end some day. For my own part, it started very vividly into life two subjecst upon which I have always found it very difficult to make a final and comprehensive decision : blood sports, and vivisection. I know quite well what my instinctive answer is to both : instant and complete condemnation. But then contributary considerations creep in, and I find myself unable to press my answer to its logical conclusion—a very distressing position for a person of logical and argumentative temper.

I have tried seriously and painfully to discover my final feelings on these matters. I care seriously about them both, for the sake of civilisation and the sake of animals. Unfortunately, the more deeply one cares, the more bad thinking one is likely to bring to the argument.

Blood-Sports

BLOOD-SPORTS is the easier problem of the two. All truly civilised men and women must recoil in horror before the scenes associated with stag-hunting and otter-hunting ; and even fox-hunting, which appeals to many either on account of the qualities it calls out in man and horse, or on account of the mischievous and unendearing character of the victim, or merely because it forms a picturesque and traditional adjunct to the country-side, meets with considerable disapproval. But are we to push our disapproval farther, and condemn also the man who takes out his gun in the hope of bagging a brace of pheasants, or the man who endeavours to deal with the nuisance of rabbits, or even the fisherman who pursues his quiet pleasure with certainly no thought of cruelty in his mind ? The answer would seem to be that we must accept a killing for necessary food, where the pursued stands at least as good a chance as the pursuer, while censuring whole-heartedly those revoltingly organised excursions on a grand scale, arranged purely for the gratification, glorification, and blood-lust of man.

Vivisection

HERE a real anguish of doubt and indecision enters my soul. Is it better to let a man suffer an obscure disease than to sacrifice a guinea-pig ? Obviously, no. Then, the principle once established, where are we to draw the line ? No one, I suppose, would deny that much valuable information has been obtained through experiments on animals, and many of us would accept without much difficulty the idea of experiments carried out as

164

humanely as possible on, say, mice and rats. (One instance of our usual bad thinking is that our sympathy varies in proportion to the size of the animal, and also in proportion to the animal's attractive or unattractive qualities.) Yet in spite of this tolerance a point must come where the most callous will boggle. A dog—your own dog —would you give him up for the advancement of science? Those trustful brown eyes, that paw laid on your knee? Supposing you saw even a photograph of him strapped down on the operating table, what would you feel then about vivisection? " But," says the surgeon, " you have admitted the principle ; to jib now is surely mere sentimentality? "

We sigh. Perhaps it is. Perhaps it is just bad thinking again that is making us so inconsistent. We know very well, however, that we have reached a ditch which we find it impossible to jump. What are we finally to concede?

We must concede that human benefit comes first ; and, having done that, assure ourselves that the precise gain to our knowledge can be acquired in no other way. Thereafter we must assure ourselves that the most stringent legislation, supported by official inspection carried out without warning, shall at least ensure that only essential experiments are undertaken, with the minimum of suffering whether mental or physical to the animal concerned. I should like to write here, more sweepingly, ' only essential and associated with the compulsory use of anæsthetics ', but I know, horrible thought, that certain brain operations can be usefully performed only during the full consciousness of the victim. I should like to write also that the more sensitive and intelligent animals should be wholly spared, but here again I fear that those better informed than I will protest that none but the highly developed subject is suitable for certain purposes. It is a grim thought. I could endure the sacrifice of frogs and rats, but there are other sacrifices which I find it impossible to contemplate.

Thus far my inconclusive reflections lead me, and at this

point I realise as I have often realised before that the only con-
structive solution I have to offer is in favour of the most severe
control and an almost unlimited judicial power of punishment.

My remarks on the quarrelsome subject of vivisection[1] resulted
(as I foresaw) in a vigorous attack of correspondence from both
the anti-vivisectionists and the research campaigners.   It provoked Mr. Bernard Shaw himself into taking up his pen.   In
fairness to both sides, I must say that each has tried to be fair to
me, even as I had tried to be fair and impartial myself, though it
is difficult to be impartial on this subject, where feeling and reason
are at even greater disaccord than usual.   It therefore seems
desirable to revive the question, and to go into it at greater
length, with, I hope, the same degree of impartiality.   I should
like to state simply and straightforwardly at the start that I love
animals as deeply as the most ardent anti-vivisectionist can, and
that the idea of their being forced to suffer on our behalf is
instinctively repugnant to me.   I hope that my word for this may
be accepted as sincerely as it is meant, and that having dispelled
all possible misunderstanding I need say no more about it.

Much, much as I should like to range myself wholly on the
side of the anti-vivisectionists I still cannot do so.   Even after
reading all their arguments, and heaving all my own feelings
into the scale on their side, I still cannot help believing that the
interests of man must come first.   It is a horrible choice to make,
but one must make it.   In making it, one postulates of course two
things :   (*a*) that the permanent alleviation of human suffering
matters more, in the long run, than the temporary pain of an
animal ;   (*b*) that the temporary pain of the animal will really
contribute to the permanent cure of human suffering.

The anti-vivisectionist disputes both these points.

---

[1] I am well aware that my use of the word ' vivisection ' is loose and
incorrect. ' Vivisection ' actually means a cutting operation carried out without
an anæsthetic, and as such was rendered illegal by Act of Parliament in 1876.
Since, however, ' vivisection ' has come to mean ' experiments on animals '
in the popular mind, I use the expression for brief convenience.

The Anti-vivisection Arguments

THE question for the opponent of vivisection splits into two parts. He has two separate arguments to advance. One argument is ethical, the other is practical. The ethical question is : Is vivisection morally justifiable ? The practical question is : Does vivisection lead to any useful results in the treatment of human pain and disease ?

Let me take these two points in their order.

First, the anti-vivisectionist considers that ' vivisection is cruel, and cruelty is either right or wrong ' ; moreover, that it ' ruins the souls of those who practise it '. None would deny the iniquity of wanton cruelty, and, indeed, such cases are forcibly punished in this country, but a scientific investigation conducted for the highest humanitarian ends can scarcely come under the same heading. The ethical aspect thus seems to me really unworthy of more than a moment's consideration.

Secondly, he denies that any benefits whatsoever have accrued to man as a result of the practice. The sweeping statements produced in support of this theory are scarcely borne out either by reasonableness or by the facts. It is idle to pretend, for instance, that insulin has had no effect on the treatment of diabetes ; that smallpox remains unaffected by vaccination ; that diphtheria resists all attempt at immunisation ; that the treatment of rickets and pernicious anæmia owes nothing to experiments on animals ; nor the understanding of antisepsis and anæsthetics (chloroform), the measurement of blood-pressure, and the administration of artificial respiration (Schafer's method). Such contentions destroy their own case by their very intransigence. All vaccines are declared to be useless ; the hypodermic syringe is ' a most dangerous practice and *one that is quite outside the provision of nature* ' (italics mine) ; vivisection is to be condemned if only because it has produced no cure for cancer ; and if certain diseases must be admitted to show a statistical diminution, the fact is to be ascribed solely to the improvement in sanitary conditions, not to any advance in medical science.

Such is the case which the anti-vivisectionist puts up, but on an examination of the facts, supported by statistics, the arguments appear to be untenable, and, in many instances, unfairly presented.

Another argument frequently advanced (again unsupported by facts) is that as animals differ so much from human beings, all experiments carried out on them are valueless as an indication, and that the only experiment of any value can be practised on a human being. The proper study of mankind, in fact, is man. Well, physicians and scientific researchers have often been willing to experiment on themselves. One has only to instance Simpson and Duncan, Edgeworth and Davy. There is nothing that I can see to prevent the convinced anti-vivisectionists of the present day from offering themselves as suitable subjects for experiment.

The Case for the Vivisectionist

STATISTICS so thoroughly dispel the theory that certain diseases (only a few of which have been enumerated above) have in no way yielded to the treatment discovered as a result of experiments on animals, that anyone interested may be referred to the printed evidence for himself. It is impossible to go into the details here in this short space, but the evidence is easily available and proves, I think beyond question, the precious life-saving gains to medical science. Another point consistently overlooked by the opposing party is the benefit to animals themselves, in the millions of cases prophylactically treated for such ravaging plagues as anthrax, rinderpest, rabies, and canine distemper. These facts once accepted, nothing remains in favour of the anti-vivisectionist's argument except (*a*) our humane, potent, and natural repugnance, and (*b*) our more rational and practical anxiety as to the actual terms of the law, and as to the way in which that law is administered.

The Cruelty to Animals Act, 1876

THE complete text of this law may be obtained, on application to the Stationery Office, for the price of 1s., and all that need be said here is that it attempts adequately to safeguard all animals used for experimental purposes against suffering either during, or subsequent on, the experiment. A further and most elaborate system of Certificates exists, concerning the grant of extra licences for specific cases, including the proviso that ' an animal found to be suffering pain which is either severe or likely to endure, shall forthwith be painlessly killed '. Lovers of dogs, cats, and horses may be relieved to learn that these animals receive special consideration. The principal query which remains in my mind after a careful study of these documents, is not whether they are adequately framed but whether they are adequately observed and enforced.

This, of course, is difficult for the layman to estimate. One can judge only by the report issued annually by the Home Office. In the report for the year 1937 I read that the total number of experiments was 918,960, and that 901 visits were paid by official inspectors, or roughly 0.1 per cent, a figure which seems to me insufficient for a sufficiently rigorous control. In fairness, however, one must add that these visits are nearly always paid without previous notice ; that an overwhelming proportion of this alarming total of close on a million experiments is taken up by nothing more serious than inoculations and hypodermic injections ; and that *in no case* has a licence been granted dispensing with the use of anæsthetics in any operation more severe than subcutaneous venesection (blood-letting).

These few remarks do not cover a quarter of the subject ; I have not, for instance, touched at all on the subsequent effects on the animal thus used for experimental purposes. In the mean-

171

time, however, it does appear that instead of trying, often emotionally and ignorantly, to thwart the efforts of medical science, we should do better to concentrate on the truly shocking and unnecessary cruelty involved in such practices as castration on farms, tail-docking, the use of steel traps, and certain forms of sport.

October

THIS is the time of year when the season changes its character ; when the early morning hours are soaked as well as radiant. How beautiful these October mornings can be, even though they spoil later in the day ! The spiders' webs veil the hedges with their miracle of fragile intricacy. The birds are singing again, in wistful reminiscence of the far-away spring. The quinces are turning golden to match the trees. The berries are redder than blood among the darkness of the yews, and they lie like gouts of blood on the grey paving stones where the thrushes have smashed them.

But it is also a time for activity, not merely for contemplation. Already the big cornfield has been ploughed up, and the furrows shine after the rain. The farmer and the gardener are both busy, the gardener perhaps the more excitable of the two, for he is more of the amateur, concerned with the creation of beauty rather than with the providing of food. Gardening is a luxury occupation ; an ornament, not a necessity, of life. The farmer is not at all concerned with the eventual beauty of his corn as a feature in the landscape, though, indeed, he gets a certain satisfaction out of it, as he leans against his gate on a summer evening, and sees his acres gently curving to the breeze. Still, beauty is not his primary aim ; the gardener's is. Fortunate gardener, who may preoccupy himself solely with beauty in these difficult and ugly days ! He is one of the few people left in this distressful world to carry on the tradition of elegance and charm. A useless member of society, considered in terms of economics, he must not be denied his rightful place. He deserves to share it, however humbly, with the painter and the poet.

173

The Garden in October

THE most noteworthy thing about gardeners is that they are always optimistic, always enterprising, and never satisfied. They are for ever planting, and for ever digging up. They always look forward to doing better than they have ever done before. " Next year . . ." they say, and even as they pronounce the words you become infected by their enthusiasm, and allow yourself to be persuaded that the garden will indeed look different, quite different, next year. Experience tells you that it never does; but how poor and disheartening a thing is experience compared with hope ! Let us continue to be sanguine even at the cost of future disillusionment. A pound's worth of plants is worth the full pound, even if ten shillings out of the pound eventually die on us. The survivors will compensate us for the failures.

This, then, is also the time of year when we take our gardens to pieces. It is a special moment in the year, when plants may safely be shifted round to new and better positions, and other plants may safely be introduced to one of those new planting schemes we had designed on paper earlier in the year. Throughout the spring and summer we had enjoyed the flowering beauty planned last May, but if (as I trust) we may be accounted true gardeners, this is the time when we can make drastic alterations and look forward to a better, different effect next spring. And so it goes always forward : scheme after scheme, dream after dream ; and although only a very poor proportion of the schemes and dreams come to fulfilment, there always remains the hope that some day some effort will fulfil itself in terms of our loveliest aspirations.

In the meantime, I shall continue to plant and shift during the months of October and November. I shall continue to think

174

that my garden will look quite different and better next year, although I know deep within my heart that it will look exactly the same to everyone except, perhaps, to me. Alone I shall be able to register that my shrubs are growing, and that the Winter-sweet I started from seed will at last begin to flower.

Sloe-Gin

ONE of the most pleasant autumnal occupations I know, is when I go into the low, warm kitchen to help to prick the sloes for the making of sloe-gin. Big bowls of sloes are waiting on the kitchen table under the light ; purple buttons heaped as generously as blackberries ; and there we sit, perched on the kitchen table, methodically punching each sloe with a fork. Then plop into bottles, to be filled up with gin and sugar ; corked, and left for six months to mature under the larder shelf. Under, not on, for they must be kept in the dark. I cannot quite explain why this occupation affords me such quiet satisfaction. It is not that I particularly like sloe-gin ; in fact, I rather dislike it as a sickly drink. But there is something about that yearly scene in the kitchen—the hanging light, the clean scrubbed table, the bowls of freshly-collected fruit, the blue-paper stacks of sugar, the cleaned bottles, and the baby cooing in its cot—all these things make me look forward to the evening when we shall once more make sloe-gin in the kitchen.

Fog

LEANING over the parapet of the Pont Neuf, I watched a few swirls of vapour drift above the river, so ethereal and milky that they really only added to the cleanliness and elegance of Paris. A Frenchman beside me thought otherwise. " Voilà," he observed gloomily to his companion, " voilà ce qu' à Londres on appelle le fog."

I was amused by this remark, having a sudden vision of a midnight darkness descending on London at midday, diabolical with flares, congested with crawling traffic. There is a certain beauty in this black-and-red effect, however, although it may be denied to the choking yellow variety ; and considerable beauty also in the white country fog, so long as it is not too thick. It must be transparent enough for us to discern the shapes of trees, their trunks cut off, so that nothing but the finely veined heads remain, untethered, as sometimes in a desert mirage the tops of mountains appear to float suspended above the solid earth. In this thin fog, familiar objects become invested with a new unreality : it is as though we were seeing them for the first time. *Dissimili non sono che nei sembianti*—a most profound remark. Even houses, the homes of men, become as suggestive as the unknown lives moving inside them. A side-road, opening and vanishing as we creep past, might lead into another and more desirable world. It is only when the shroud really comes down and we know that the thickening must deepen with the failing daylight, that fog turns into the enemy, obliterating, instead of enchanting, our way.

Since such disadvantages are likely, indeed certain, to overwhelm our island at intervals during six months of every year, upsetting the arrangements of thousands and even throwing them into actual danger, why may we not be given white kerb-stones

along our country roads ? The device is obvious and relatively
inexpensive. There would be no need for the extravagance of a
running kerb everywhere ; white, painted, upright stones, like
miniature milestones, placed every few yards would be of enormous value to the motorist in fog. One knows the difficulty of
trying to follow a grass verge ; one knows also with what relief
one hails a mere white central line. Now in Italy, where the
peril of fog is practically nil, many of the main roads and bridges
are ornamented by black and white striped stones, running for
miles, for no reason that I can see except pure *bravura*. If Italy
can afford this luxury, why can we in England not afford a similar
necessity ?

Sylva Cœdua

A SMALL imitator of fog appears in autumn, not only in the early morning mists, but also in the smoke of bonfires burning (most uneconomically) leaves, haulms, and rubbish. The skill of the born countryman in building a fire out of the dampest material, a fire which will smoulder for days, even under rain, is an art which has to be learnt ; it may not be so exact as the art of the charcoal-burner, who day and night must temper his pile to the wind, but it is ingenious enough. Very soon now an extra coil of bluer smoke will rise above the woods, and drift across the brown and yellow trees in that slow imperceptibly spreading way to which no other pace is comparable : it means that the wood-

cutters are at work. Already the auctions of underwood have
taken place in the local sale-rooms, and the underwood has been
knocked down at sums varying from under five to perhaps twenty
pounds an acre—it depends on the size and variety of the wood,
but in any case provides an easy and recurrent income for the
landowner. Chestnut ranks high for spiles, poles, and fencing ;
birch comes much lower down, being no longer required for such
purposes as the yokes of oxen, and finding very little use now save
for children's toys, brooms, and handles. In Kent we reckon our
wood by the cant, meaning the area between one ride and the
next ; I had always taken this term for granted, but realised that
it must be a local expression when a sudden qualm made me look
it up in the big *Oxford Dictionary* to discover that even in
that majestic work it was not recorded in this connexion.
Our local woodmen, I observed, sometimes refer to it as a
canter.

Coppice planting has a respectable ancestry, dating back to
1543 under the Statute of Woods, with subsequent encouragements.
The first time I ever ordered a cant to be cut, I did so with
dreadful misgivings, for I hate the sound of axe on wood, but now
I welcome the annual arrival of the wood-cutters in my own
woods, knowing that it will not impair but rather will enhance
their beauty. From beginning to end the process is one long
delight. I like to see the tree-trunks appearing suddenly in their
naked couthness, and the ground exposed with all its system of
rabbit-burries, hitherto concealed. I like the primitive traditional
shelters that the men put up for their labours—four poles at the
corners, and a roof of brushwood or canvas, looking oddly ' native '
in the woods of Kent. I like the rude mallets and tripods that they
fashion from the material lying ready to hand. I like the quick
skill with which they perform their work—the sharp slanting cut
as low as possible, since tall cutting means gnarled stools ten or
twelve years hence, and rough, unskilful cutting means rotting
stools. I like knowing that, next spring, bluebells and foxgloves

will appear in the clearings, where I have never seen them before.

I like the men themselves, with their wise store of woodcraft and wood-knowledge. There is one whole family which works on its own account in my wood, from half-past six in the morning till half-past six in the evening, a father, mother, and six children. Four of the children are under school-age, and their parents bring them every day to sleep or tumble under the trees, brown little woodland cubs, while the handsome young man and woman fell, slice, strip, and stack the redolent wood ; during the holidays the two elder children come too, almost as skilful at stripping the bark, industrious, and apparently indefatigable. They have their moments of relaxation, though every half-hour spent in play means a loss of earned pennies. But no child could resist the toy left at their disposal. Someone had dumped an old car among the undergrowth, lacking wheels or engine, a black, disreputable object which came to light as the chestnut began to fall around it, so incongruously reminiscent of the American Middle West that I resolved crossly to get it removed at the first opportunity. Next time I passed that way, five happy urchins were scrambling in and out of it, going for imaginary rides, calling a halt, putting the baby in the dickey, getting in again, imitating the horn (which was missing), starting off again for a new destination.

Finally, I like feeling that the woods are being properly used. I like the idea that the man (whoever he was), who planted the coppices in such orderly rows, is now looking down with approval from some better place, seeing that his plantings are regularly attended to every ten to fourteen years. He must have made his plantings at least a hundred years ago, and I hope he does not feel that he has secured too unworthy or too unappreciative a successor.

All these things deeply satisfy my incurably Tory soul.

November

FACTS so often disprove the theory that November is an unpleasant month that I begin to wonder whether the theory was ever well-founded, or whether our climate is actually changing. This year, apart from a few days of particularly savage gales, November has been as mild as spring, the thermometer sometimes nearly touching 70 in the shade. One notices such things in the country more closely than in cities, especially if one has a garden and consignments of shrubs and bulbs waiting to be planted in it. I understand that I share this innocent taste with some five million of my compatriots, and that between us we spend some forty million pounds annually on our gardens. It is satisfactory to think how obligingly the weather has behaved towards so large and extravagant a number of us.

Fashions in gardening change, not owing only to caprice or the prevailing taste but owing also to the increasing choice of plants placed upon the market. Take, for example, the many varieties of flowering trees now available, pyrus or prunus, I doubt whether the average amateur bothers to differentiate much between the ever-changing classifications. The main point is, that he can now secure them at reasonable prices, and plants them freely in his garden. Many of them are relatively new— the Japanese cherry itself made its appearance only at the end of last century in this country—and consequently few full-grown specimens are to be seen as yet except, say, at Kew or in the private gardens of certain pioneers. For most of us, they are still represented only by spindly little trees with the nurseryman's orange label still fluttering. It pleases me to reflect how superb the heads of blossom will be in fifteen or twenty years' time. Some villages even planted avenues to commemorate the Coronation ; one can predict that the whole aspect of these villages will be changed when the trees have had time to grow, forcing the descendant of Herr Baedeker to add a note drawing attention to this remarkable feature in his Guide to England for 1950.

Wind-monath

APART from the pleasures of gardening, November has beauty of its own. The Saxons called it the wind-month, for then the fishermen drew up their boats and abandoned fishing till the spring ; it was called the slaughter-month, too, when pigs and cattle were salted down for preservation throughout the winter. Scarcely affected by this precaution to-day, we still can think of it as the wind-month which brings the last leaf off the tree. It is not a bad test of a person, to discover whether he sees as much (perhaps more) beauty in the naked boughs as in the obvious loveliness in June. To his discerning eye the ploughed field will seem as noble as the corn, and infinitely more austere. If it is a bare month, it is also a busy one. Man is busy, with his eternal optimism preparing for next year ; and the squirrels, too, are busy in their less longsighted way, preparing merely to get through the winter. I went out early one morning, so early that I wasn't expected by the small occupants of the orchard, and flung a squirrel into a rage and a couple of wood-pigeons into taking their blundering flight out of a pear-tree. I could not be sure whether the squirrel blamed the disturbance on the pigeons, or whether the pigeons blamed it on the squirrel, or whether they all blamed it on me. Anyhow, there I was, out in the orchard before I was expected, upsetting everybody at an hour when they thought they might have the orchard to themselves. The pigeons set off on their heavy clumsy flight, the squirrel rushed up his tree, chattering with anger. I followed him, and sighted his drey, untidily built of leaves, in the fork of an oak tree overhanging the moat. I could have shot him dead there and then, and indeed the law tells me to do so ; he is a mischievous little beast, I know, but somehow when I saw him preparing his winter larder, even though I guessed it to be stocked chiefly with my own precious

nuts, I could not have brought my finger to press the trigger.
This was sheer sentimentality on my part, for both reason and
the law assure me that the grey squirrel ought to be exterminated.
Of course, I prefer the red squirrel, and liked once to see him
leaping about our woodlands ; I know also that the grey, the
alien tree-rat, is supposed to have ousted him, though this is a
moot point ; but somehow I cannot bring myself to shoot so
nimble and pretty a little beast. The very rush he makes up the
tree into safety, his chattering angry cry, compensate me for the
loss of many nuts. That early hour in the orchard, when I sur-
prised him and the wood-pigeon, meant more to me than many
bushels, whether of cob or filbert. Such moments bring one into
a closer communion with the secret life of nature than any amount
of reading in even the most sympathetic books.

Fox-hunting

RECENTLY the local Hunt drew a covert neighbouring my own small estate. I heard the familiar shouts, and the deep note of the hounds, and went to the top of my tower to watch the whole procedure. From there I could observe the beauty and picturesqueness of that remarkably English scene, the pink coats moving among the brown underwood, the skewbald hounds ranging eagerly, the tossing heads of horses as the followers waited near a gate. If only they had been pursuing a drag, I thought, how happily I could have given myself up to enjoyment ! They found their fox, however, when to my delight he had the sense to bolt straight into my own private wood where the Hunt is forbidden to follow. A hunt-servant on a white horse galloped off to recover some couples of hounds, and I reflected, not without pleasure, on what my neighbours must be saying about me. Nothing would disturb that fox now, so long as he remained where he was, nothing worse than a big waggon lumbering down to bring in the cord-wood for my fires. He would not grudge me that. Meanwhile the discomfited field moved off, and I came down from the tower, leaving the wild bees that have lived up there for generations to their winter sleep.

Sudden Snowfall

LOOKING out of my window early on the shortest day of the year, I observed a large hay-wain pursuing its way across the big meadow—no uncommon sight, when one lives in the middle of a farm. A familiar sight indeed : the trusses piled clumsily high, the team pulling sturdily, the two men trudging alongside, their upright whips drawn delicately against the sky. The world, however, had turned white during the night.

It was dazzlingly white in sunlight, and across the virgin snow the haycart toiled on its way, looking absurdly out of place. The nostrils of the horses smoked, as like a great black ship the heavy cart lurched and rocked on its way between the rick and the cow-sheds. In the complete stillness of this quilted world it was the only thing that moved.

There was no colour at all, nothing but a photographic black and white, or so it seemed at first sight, until one noticed that the white pigeons sitting on the roof of the barn were really electric blue. The pigeons reminded me of the birds, which must be hungry, and going downstairs I found them hopping in dozens on the platform where they are accustomed to find their food. Usually one perceives birds separately, and at a distance, but the advantage of perches at eye-level just outside the window is that they come in congregations, their collective colours brilliant and varied as a paint-box. Blue-tits, great-tits, chaffinches, robins, all bright morsels flying, hopping, picking, perching, dangling, flashing in the snow, far more vivid than when the world was green. Their behaviour was not at all in accordance with their loveliness. The robins, driven by hunger, had forgotten to be as disagreeable as usual ; but a large throstle, after eating his fill, took up his position and with clapping beak turned the platform into a kind of Tom Tiddler's ground, where the small fry could

187

snatch only at their peril. Self-satisfaction spread over me as I considered how far more charitable I was being than they to their own kind. In fact, there are few occupations which induce greater self-satisfaction than dispensing food to hungry birds. Their need is so great, and one's own wealth so boundless. One does not know whether to feel more like St. Francis or Lord Nuffield, but either persuasion is flattering. The maize I threw out to the pigeons turned into golden sovereigns as it left my hands. And not only food but warmth is miraculously at one's disposal. A half-dead wagtail, gradually reviving, wrapped in flannel near the fire ; a dove sitting on the back of a chair ; and in my own sitting-room a robin (he must have come down the chimney), perching with complete assurance and an innate sense of decoration among the jade leaves and coral berries of a Chinese tree. He stayed with me while the snow lasted, and with the thaw I let him go.

Traps in the Snow

MY sense of loving-kindliness, however, exaggerated as it was by the season and by the resources of charity at my command, had been disturbed by the wickedness of the throstle, which affected me much as the pea affected the princess. It may have been a small thing to come as a reminder of the cruelty of nature, whether human or otherwise ; a small thing, in a world where the nastier qualities may be observed daily on so extensive a scale. Men were killing one another in China and Spain, and preparing possibly to kill one another in Europe also ; but somehow that vicious little snap of the throstle's beak, that dog-in-the-manger attitude of the already gorged bird, shocked me as closely as anything I could read that morning in the daily paper—a disproportionate sensibility, no doubt, but none the less real. It made me wonder how deep true kindliness could go ; how ill-considered it really was ; how shallow, how easily dispelled. The English, I reflected, were on the whole a mild and kindly race ; they disliked violence, they were amiably and even sentimentally disposed towards animals and children ; the cases prosecuted by the R.S.P.C.A. were the exception, not the rule. I remembered an occasion when I gave orders for a litter of mongrel puppies to be drowned, and then met the gardener, carefully sheltering the puppies under his coat from the rain, on his way to plunge them all into a bucket of water. " I wouldn't like the poor little chaps to get wet," he explained.

Is this hypocrisy, or merely bad thinking ? It is useless to draw the moral, but useful to dwell on the results. How, for example, can we continue to countenance a practice which allows an animal, be it rabbit, fox, or dog, to twist its broken paw out of a steel trap between the hours of sunset and sunrise ? Few men, I think, would stand by and watch such agony, yet many cheerfully make such agony possible. Lack of imagination, I suppose. What the eye does not see, the heart does not suffer. But we ought not to be content to leave it at that.

A Country Party

AN elegant pamphlet written by a Mr. Cornell in 1814 brought me some warming thoughts on a cold morning. The title in itself was genial : *A treatise calculated for making excellent wines from the various fruits of this United Country, in relation to strength, brilliancy, health and economy*. It had distressed Mr. Cornell that ' so many a Mr. and Mrs. Bull ' should be hoaxed with foreign wines, which were not only exorbitantly expensive but perniciously doctored, when such wines as juniper, whortle-berry, cowslip, mead, and metheglin could be made in the still-room and matured in the cellar. The author approaches his subject with a suitable reverence ; vinous fermentation, to him, is ' a divine operation which the Omniscient Creator has placed in our cup of life ' ; the idea that wines should not be given fair play, but should be drunk before they have attained their full beauty, strength and fragrance, rouses him to indignation. How, he asks, can individuals expect their wines to be good and generous if drunk in such improper circumstances ? When, however, he hears the seething in his own vats (in which he has been careful to place a mysterious object he calls a huc-muc) his satisfaction is such that he can relieve his feelings only by a homely comparison : it is puffing and blowing, he says, like our old cart-horse.

At last the great moment arrived when he could invite a party of friends to celebrate his vintage of three hundred gallons. The company included the author's Aunt Hambleton, the sprightly Widow Conway, the Reverend Mr. Rubicund, Miss Wood, a young lady to whom the occasion was especially interesting as she was on the point of being led to the hymeneal altar by young Farmer Moam ; and Miss Jurtina Meadows, whom Mr. Cornell ' had dignified with the classic appellation of Sappho, since in her unbending moments she wrote stanzas terse and chastely sapphic '.

They were all very gay. Miss Meadows especially appears to

have been enjoying one of her unbending moments, for Mr. Cornell records that ' a radiation was playing between mine and the blue eye of Jurtina ', and towards the end of the evening it was she who observed that since the ancients did celebrate their vintages with dance and song, the moderns might well follow their example. She had brought her pedal harp with her ; touching it now ' with delicacy and Attic grandeur ' she proposed a song from each in turn. The company being very ready to oblige, Mr. Grimston led off with *The Brave British Soldier*, followed by the Widow Conway with *I Sigh for a Husband at Sixty*, accompanying the stanzas with such sportive winks and blinks that a lover would have lowered her age full 20 per cent. Mr. Rubicund then sang *The Bower of Felicity*, not once, but twice, his nose by that time being highly tinged with purple. Aunt Hambleton tried next, but broke down ; she ' made an attempt to sing a little rural song, but her memory was not equal to her inclination ', and Mrs. Moam, having neither pipe nor song, had likewise to be excused.

Jurtina came to the rescue. Fixing her host with her blue eye, she melodiously sang a little pastoral of her own composition in which the following verse occurred :

> How delightful his vineyard, his cot,
> Where rational amusements combine.
> Oh ! how happy would indeed be my lot
> Could I say to myself, *He is mine*.

Lively, elegant Jurtina. She now proceeded to create Bacchanalian Personages : the Rev. Rubicund was High Priest, the ladies were Arcadian Nymphs, she herself was the Goddess Ariadne, and their host of course was enthroned as Bacchus in a great arm-chair decorated with ivy and laurel.

It was impossible, he said, to describe their mirth and glee. His cup was full (in more ways, I suspect, than one), when on bidding him good-night Jurtina embraced his hand with the tenderest affection, whispering in his ear, " Call me no longer Sappho, but your—Ariadne ! "

'And the Stranger within thy Gates'

SHE arrived in a wooden crate, labelled with the word 'Worcester', so I called her Worcester, knowing her by no other name. There exists in history a reputable tradition by which people may take their surname from the town of their origin, so being unable to discover her personal name from the gentleman who had been so kind as to supply her at my request, I called her after the station from which he had dispatched her. A simple reason, but quite a good one. I could scarcely have received her as a guest under my roof for six or eight weeks, and left her anonymous all that time. That would have been not only inconvenient, but also inhospitable and impolite.

The gentleman who supplied me with Worcester employed the most delightful writing-paper ; unlike most writing-paper it did not confine itself to a bald statement of the address, but in addition was copiously illustrated. It was sprinkled with diminutive reproductions of photographs, all apparently taken between 1880 and 1890. There was one of the gentleman himself, or possibly his father, dressed in a black coat and a bowler hat, holding a litter of lion-cubs in his arms. There was another of a lady and a little girl, holding baby bears. There was another of a retriever bitch with young tigers crawling over her. Even the retriever, stout and complacent, managed to convey unmistakably the later Victorian period.

Worcester herself was completely Victorian, both as to appearance and character. More of a sheep-dog than anything else, though doubtless other elements were present, she resembled one of those woolly hearthrugs which lay before the big coal fire in Victorian drawing-rooms. Her grey coat was matted, her face

193

round as an owl's, her tail a mere bob, her paws chubby. Her nature was made for integral and unquestioning devotion, a devotion which for those few weeks, from the first moment, she chose to lavish upon me. I loved Worcester almost as much as Worcester loved me, yet how badly I treated her! No cad ever behaved worse to the woman who loved him. First I hired her, unseen, unknown, for my own selfish convenience, for a paltry sum too, a mere three guineas plus travelling expenses. Then I took her children, the four blind puppies she had brought with her, and caused them to be drowned one by one, day by day, in a bucket. It is true that owing to her conjugal carelessness they were worthless mongrels; true also that I replaced them one by one by aristocratic Alsatians of the same age; but they were her own and she whimpered a little each time I removed one. Yet how kindly she took to her fosterlings! There was nothing of the stepmother about her as she nuzzled those four little wolfish cubs in the straw and gave them the best she had to give—her care, her warmth, and her milk. Her pride in them was as great as if they had been her own; she never suspected that they were only four out of a litter of eight, given over to her because eight were too many for their own mother to feed.

Nor did she know that their mother, my own savagely jealous bitch, would have fallen on her and torn her soft body to rags had she suspected her presence. I kept them very carefully apart, the mother in the kennel, Worcester in her shed. I let Worcester out only when the Alsatian was safely shut away. Then Worcester came lumbering out, happy to be free, happy to be with me in the garden, but always so conscientious about her charges that she would make sudden dashes back to the shed, make sure that they were safe, and then gallop back to me, reassured.

Then her time began to draw towards its end. The little wolves were growing beyond her, and as they started to snarl and bicker she would look at them with a slightly puzzled air. They were learning to lap from a bowl and were becoming rough, with a roughness that was never inherited from a sheep-dog. And as they grew daily more independent and more fierce, so did Worcester transfer more and more of her large loving heart to me. They might not need her any longer, but she had decided that I did. So she sat beside me as I gardened, and though I encouraged her to rummage round for mice and rabbits and to have a little fun in return for the service she had rendered me, she would not stir. She merely looked at me with her good brown eyes gazing through her shaggy face, and scraped at my hand with an enormous paw, as though she were saying, " Don't send me away. Let me stay. This is my happiness."

I knew, however, more and more miserably I knew it, that I should soon have to send her away. If I had kept her openly she would have got murdered, and I couldn't permanently play this game of Box and Cox between the kennel and the shed. And surely my first loyalty was due to the beautiful intransigent creature who had two years' claim to oppose to Worcester's seven weeks, two years during which she had regarded me as her exclusive property? No, Worcester must return to her career. The professional foster-mother. Litter after litter of mongrel puppies, drowned one by one to make room for small strangers of champion stock. Employer after employer, all base, all treacherous, all paying their three guineas, all accepting Worcester's love and service, all lifting Worcester back into her empty crate on the last morning. . . .

Gadgets

I MISTRUST gadgets, generally speaking. They seldom work. The proved, old-fashioned tool is usually better and it is safer to stick to it. I thus make a rule of throwing all tempting catalogues of gardening gadgets straight into the waste-paper basket, not daring to examine them first, because I know that if I examine them I shall fall. It will mean only that I shall with some trouble obtain a postal order for 10s. 6d., to acquire an object which will speedily join similar objects rusting in the tool shed. It should be clear from this that my mistrust of gadgets is equalled only by my weakness for them, and that no amount of experience can make me find them anything but irresistible.

Nevertheless this attitude may be ungrateful, for there are certain gadgets which have been my companions for so long that I have ceased to think of them under that name. There is the walking-stick shaped like a golf-club with a cutting edge to slash down thistles ; you can do it without pausing as you walk, and not only does it control the thistles but provides a harmless outlet for ill-temper. Then there is the long narrow trowel of stainless steel and its associate the two-pronged hand fork, both unrivalled for weeding in between small plants, though perhaps there is no tool so well adapted for this purpose as the old table knife with the stump of a broken blade. There is the little wheel on the long handle, like a child's toy, which you push before you and which twinkles round, cutting the verge of the grass as it goes. Above all, there is the widger, the neatest, slimmest, and cheapest of all gadgets to carry in the pocket. Officially the widger is Patent No. 828793, but it owes (I believe) its more personal name to the ingenuity of Mr. Clarence Elliott, whose racy gardening style ought to be more widely appreciated. He invented the widger, its name, and the verb to widge, which, although not exactly

onomatopœic, suggests very successfully the action of prising up—
you widge up a weed, or widge up a caked bit of soil for the
purpose of ærating it—all very necessary operations which before
the arrival of the widger were sometimes awkward to perform.
This small sleek object, four inches long, slides into the pocket, no
more cumbersome than a pencil, and may be put to many uses.
Screwdriver, toothpick, letter-opener, widger, it fulfils all functions
throughout the day. Its creator, Mr. Elliot, I observe, spells it
sometimes with a ' y ' : wydger, no doubt on the analogy of
Blake's Tyger, just to make it seem more unusual. Whatever
the spelling, it is the perfect gadget.

What an odd little word ' gadget ' is, almost a gadget in itself,
so small and useful. Its origin is obscure and it is believed not to
appear in print before 1886. Yet it is not, as might be thought,
an Americanism. It appears as an expression used chiefly by
seamen, meaning any small tool, contrivance, or piece of
mechanism not dignified by any specific name ; a what-not, in
fact ; a chicken-fixing, a gill-guy, a timmey-noggy, a wim-wom.
I commend these agreeable synonyms to Mr. Clarence Elliott's
notice, and at the same time record my gratitude for his revival
of that other sea-faring word, manavlins. I wonder how many
English-speaking people are familiar with its meaning ?

Tool-shed

DIFFERENT from gadgets are the time-honoured tools which hang in the dusty brown twilight of the tool-shed when their day's work is done. The wood of their handles is as tawny as the arms of the men who use them ; they have a sun-burnt air. The steel of spuds, forks, and trowels glistens quietly as though it were resting ; it has been in contact with the earth all day, and recalls the old expedient of plunging a dirty knife-blade into the soil and withdrawing it restored to a brightness like the flash of Excalibur. The prongs of forks are burnished as bayonets, the curve of hooks gleaming as sabres. The big wooden trugs repose peacefully across the handles of the barrow. The long handles of rakes and hoes dangle in rows, symmetrical as Uccello's lances. There is a shelf with all the odd accumulation of labels, green string, hedging-gloves, old tobacco tins full of saved seeds. A hank of yellow bass hangs from a nail, blond as corn. The flower-pots are piled, tier upon tier, red as a robin's breast. Red and brown, green and golden, steely as armour, dusty as snuff, the tool-shed deepens in shadow as the respite of evening shuts the door and leaves the small interior to the mouse.

Note from another Country: Burgundy

IT seems remarkable that English tourists should penetrate so sparsely into provincial France—English tourists, who have but to hop across the Channel, a light matter for Englishmen who cannot afford to fear the sea.

The Channel is a different matter for such Europeans as may enjoy a whole continent spread around them, and may take a train from one station to another without facing the discomfort of boats and an element which takes no account of passengers, whether *de luxe* or third class. How often has one heard, on foreign lips, the words ' *Je crains la mer* ', and how impossible do these words become, translated into the English idiom! The continent of Europe is overrun with English men and women who have not feared the sea.

Provincial France is the surprising exception. A few cars bearing the G.B. disc draw up before the Hôtel de l'Europe at Avignon ; others stop to lunch at Chartres ; the *châteaux* of the Loire open their doors to the descendants of the nation who burnt Joan of Arc ; but in the little French towns and country districts you will not find them. A stray undergraduate with a knapsack may follow Stevenson across the Cevennes, but the great tide has not yet flowed up into the backwaters. One rejoices ; but one wonders why.

La belle France—the very words are tender, opulent, and embosoming. They imply a generous rolling country watered by many streams, softened by many forests, enriched by cornfields and vineyards, studded with little cities fat and rich with the memorials of secular history and art. Those who see only the open hedgeless plains of the north between Calais and Paris, or

201

the scorched horizons of Provence on the way to the Riviera, have
no idea of the bounty concealed within the folds of the secluded
regions.   Yet the provinces of France are easily accessible—such
provinces as Burgundy, for instance, where you are in the depths
of the French country, as rich as the wine it produces, among the
towns of lovely names : Avalon, Auxerre, Vézelay.   What more
could anybody want ?

Vézelay is a village, twelve miles from a station ; a steep
village crowning a hill, and crowned in its turn by the cathedral
which dominates all the surrounding country like the Ark marooned
on Ararat when the floods had retreated.   Vineyards pour down
the hill-side, and the sunset from the ramparts is like spilt red
wine over the voluptuous curves of the landscape.   Down at the
foot of a hill winds a river between poplars, among the woods
and the water-meadows, with cattle standing knee-deep in the
shallows.

It is all on a large and placid scale, as placid as the great
creamy oxen who sway along the lanes dragging waggon-loads of
timber behind them.   The sense of a deep, old, country existence
is everywhere present, both civic and agricultural, for the little
towns are but the fitting complement of the quiet peasant life ;
they have been for centuries the rallying-point of the men who
come into them occasionally for market or for worship.   The
fields for labour ; the market-place for barter ; the cathedral for
religion.

It is never possible to forget that this is a Catholic country.
The doors of the churches are always open, the churches seldom
empty.   One or two figures kneel in the shadows of a side-chapel,
and the whisper of confession rustles like a bird that seeks its way
out.   The dim interior is pervaded by the scent of recent incense,
and the little lamp hangs burning in reminder of the vitality of
Rome.   The light filters through the stained glass that is a glory
of France ; through the windows of Auxerre, Bourges, and
Chartres, and once of Rheims.   The church is dark, and the glow

of the coloured light comes through as though the windows were made of the petals of many flowers.

That is the quality of stained glass ; it seems to be made of living substance. Its peculiar vital brilliance makes paint seem thick and dead. For this reason the most beautiful windows, to my mind, are those which restrict themselves to pattern without any attempt at representation ; the kaleidoscope effect of pure design, apparently haphazard though in reality exquisitely balanced and proportioned, is ideally adapted to such fragments of splendour. The leaded lines which unite them interrupt no such continuity as we demand for, say, the representation of a human figure ; but rather add, by their blackness, to the illusion of a slab of many colours, smashed to pieces and put together again between us and the light. This, I think, is the particular property of stained glass. The telling of a story, the portrayal of a scene, is not its function ; that may be left to paint and canvas, tempera and fresco. Stained glass delights us with the pure and primitive pleasure of pattern ; of pattern which springs up suddenly, like a jet, amidst the gravity of stone ; a sudden exuberance breaking the exactions of architecture, piercing the solid wall with fantasy like an exaltation of the heart on an ordinary day ; yet rich with a deep sobriety, not merely light-heartedly gay.

Coming out from the church, it is pleasant to sit or stroll beneath the plane trees which, regularly planted, provide an outdoor room roofed with green in the heart of the town ; or to idle through the streets, paying tribute to the French genius for domestic architecture. The streets are quiet and sunny, but their sleepiness is diversified by many a stone balcony of baroque swagger, or pointed turret at the edge of the town overhanging the drop above some wooded valley. You may even find a fair, where it is possible not only to enjoy the spectacle of a lively nation amusing itself, but also to purchase many delightful and unusual objects.

I remember such a fair at Saulieu in Burgundy, with a merry-go-round whose wooden horses were not horses at all, but pigs and swans and prancing dragons with scarlet nostrils ; and a Bal Tabarin where the gipsies as well as the peasants of the neighbour-hood had congregated ; and a travelling circus whose performance I refused to watch because I do not like to see lions made to jump through paper hoops. The fair came to life in the evening, when flares illuminated its tinsel gaiety and wherever one walked one was showered with confetti. But even during the day-time it was not void of interest, for then the little booths displayed their wares ; and, succumbing to the perennial temptation of buying something in an out-of-the-way place, something which would have a sentimental value once one had got it home, however trashy it might then appear, I bought a blue glass bottle embossed with all the marks of punctuation—comma, asterisk, query, semi-colon—for which I might surely have scoured all the pawnbrokers of England in vain. I wondered then and wonder still, for what market a bottle decorated with the marks of punctuation could possibly be made ? Then one could buy coats of olive-green corduroy with every button different, buttons bearing such emblems of sport as a pheasant, a partridge, a hare, a stag, *garde-de-chasse* coats, which would have made the envy of our English poacher.

It is surprising how a few days dawdling in a village will familiarise one with its life. By the second morning one already recognises the butcher's dog, the grocer's errand-boy, the village cripple. One knows at what hour to expect the postman on his rounds, to listen for the bell calling the children back to school. Living in such a place one readily assumes an attitude of superiority towards birds of passage. One is a Resident, impatient for the luncheon-hour invasion to pass on with a roar of cut-outs, leaving the village street to its siesta and oneself to a life which has already arranged itself into the grooves of habit.

One regards the invaders with an amused though slightly

irritable contempt, forgetting that only yesterday one arrived oneself by the Paris train, and that next week another train will carry one away from this tiny focus of one's brief adoption.

Note from another Country: French Savoy

THE village itself lies at the meeting-place of two green valleys ;
it straddles across the river, and its grey stone houses match
the boulders that have rolled down from the heights into the
meadows. So green are the valleys, so lush the grass, that this
would seem to be a place of the soft lowlands ; it is only on
looking up that you notice the line of the larches, which stop as
though they had been artificially planted, and remember that you
stand in fact at a height of over six thousand feet. Then you
begin to wonder, and to inquire ; you look at the peasants, in
blouses and straw hats, scything the grass and the flowers in
the full blaze of the sun, with summer hanging so heavily over
everything as almost to persuade the stranger that he has come
to a hot southern climate ; and in the heat of the day there occurs
to you the thought, as a spectre arising, that in the winter months
the valley must present a very different aspect. . . .

The peasants smile when you ask them. Yes, they say :
from June to September, that is our summer, from the feast of
St. John (June 24th) to the feast of St. Michael (September 29th).
Those are the dates when the cows first go out to pasture, and
when they finally return. And little by little, thanks to your
questioning, you find out what sort of winter this is, which lasts
for nine months of the year. Snow over everything, and the
wind howling down the valleys, and no communication with the
outside world save on skis or sleighs. All outdoor work ceases ;
there is nothing to do but huddle indoors, the men repairing their
tools and carts, the women making lace and knitting stockings,
all living in one room with their cattle.

I saw one such room in the house of the village muleteer ; a

low, dark room full of shadows, the beds sunk into the walls like cupboard shelves, curtained off ; six cow-stalls down one side, and a smell of clean stable. The small, mouse-coloured cows stood munching their supper, looking as though they were made of suède, and filling the room with their gentle shifting and breathing. It was very easy to believe in the comfort that the warmth of their bodies could give in winter.

The curé himself, in whose house I lodged, shared his quarters with his cow. She lived in a room on the ground floor, her name was Marquise, and she used the front door like a lady. The curé, Marquise, and their servant, Theodorine, made up the household between them. In winter they carried the portable range from the kitchen into Marquise's room—I scarcely like to call it her stable—lived there, ate there, and slept there, all three of them. How that household would have rejoiced Balzac ! and how he would have appreciated all the inhabitants of the village, from the abbé in his skull-cap and green velveteen suit, who had once lived in Paris and was now returned to end his days in his birth-place, to Mademoiselle in the post office who could be heard bullying the entire province on the telephone. Above all, how Balzac would have appreciated Madame X.

Madame X kept the hotel, but she was more than an hotel-keeper ; she was a Napoleon. That woman knows as much about life as she does about cooking. She does not spend the whole of her year in the Val ; with the onset of winter she shuts up her hotel and retires to Paris ; but what she does in Paris is a mystery which nobody has yet fathomed. All that concerns her guests in the Val is that she concentrates upon her business as though she had no other pre-occupation in the world. Stout, motherly, bustling, capable, she contrived to give each guest the impression that she had taken him or her under her protection. The most surly and close-cropped of mountaineers did not long remain surly, for she could charm a smile out of the most recalcitrant Prussian. She would come round, at dinner, bearing an enormous basin of whipped cream, as proud as an artist with his achievement. " Voilà quelque chose qui vous rendra vos forces, mon petit enfant ", she would say to the poor little dyspeptic who sat among his medicine bottles at the next table. Her relations with her guests were purely personal, and although she no doubt had her favourites it was difficult to discover who they were. Her persuasiveness had but one drawback : one ate too much. Partly to please her, since she looked so really distressed if one refused a second helping, partly because of the excellence of what she set before one. " Madame, may I take my lunch out to-morrow ? " And there would be a basket prepared, with cold chicken (*poularde de Bresse*), tomatoes, cheese, apricots, and peaches. Then one would set off, climbing up by the cattle-tracks at first, till even those petered out, and one found oneself above the line of trees, in complete, high solitude, on the slopes of short grass blowing with the bright Alpine flowers.

Up there, it was possible to walk for the whole day without meeting a soul, or to lie by the shores of some little lake without fear of disturbance even by a shepherd. Streams abounded, and waterfalls, so that one was seldom without the pleasure of running water. Indeed, such simple delights as had been provided for the wanderer had been provided on a lavish scale. Simple they might be, but they were unsparing. This is the especial gift of mountain country : all niggardliness is absent. So noble and generous are the mountains themselves that their humbler complements seem anxious to follow their example. Not one stream, but twenty streams ; not a dozen flowers, but thousands of flowers ; no dubious hazy sun, but the sun in uninterrupted glory. Parsimony in all its forms is put to shame.

The flowers above all excelled themselves in variety and abundance. At first sight the hill-sides seemed to be indiscriminately peopled with them, but on closer observation they resolved themselves into a multitude of tiny separate gardens, planned and selected with the nicest art. Within the circles of

scattered boulders they grouped themselves according to their habit : the rosy, cushioned silene pressed close against.the rock, the grassy cup starred with mauve violas and the blue of the gentian. What tantalisation for the gardener ! he who at home, and with endless trouble, persuades a few trumpets of gentian to face the damp English spring, and who here beholds them thrown about in handfuls over acres of turf. How amazing are their brilliance and their delicacy ! they grow with no fear of the imposing summits around them, these bright tiny things, intimidated neither by the space and, emptiness nor by the storms which stalk over these lonely heights, the lightning dancing along the ground, for these are the places where the elements have things to themselves—but seeming rather to be the natural children of this large austerity, small, lucent, daring, the only colour vividly dashed on the green monotone of the turf below the rocky or the snowy peaks.

And—since the pursuit of flowers leads us always higher and higher ; since we are soon no longer content with the gentians and violas, but must seek for rarer and more fastidious things—it is remarkable how, the higher you climb, the more delicate become the flowers. You would imagine that they should become more robust as the altitude becomes more severe, but the reverse is true : down in the valleys the coarser flowers mix with the grasses, and are scythed down with them to make fodder for the cattle ; it is up on the high passes that you find the flowers which best please the fastidious taste. Between nine and ten thousand feet, exposed to all the anger of heaven, you find *Androsace alpina* and *Potentilla nitida*, tight against the shale, growing as low against the earth as any plant possibly could grow, rooted in stone as it seemed, and drawing its colour apparently from nothing but some bleakly geological substance, since soil there was none ; nothing but crumbled rock ; a tiny denizen, infinitely brave. Such flowers are the small valiant children of the peaks.

Over one of these passes, they say, once came camels. A rich

merchant of Venice, a native of the Savoyard Valley anxious to revisit his birthplace before his death, set out from Italy with a caravan of camels and descended by the Col de L'Iseran upon the astonished village of Val d'Isere. That was in the sixteenth century, the caravan handsomely furnished with such trappings of harness and tassels as were a suitable accompaniment to the splendour of a wealthy Venetian in that sumptuous age. No doubt it amused him to cut a dash such as had never been seen among the poor peasants of his mountain home. The splay feet of camels slouched across the turf amongst these Alpine flowers. I see nothing inherently impossible in the story. I have myself encountered camels on passes in Asia, as high and as storm-swept as the passes of French Savoy. Camels are disagreeable but long-suffering beasts, streaming out most decoratively on a sky-line. I like to think that a caravan of camels came once from Venice to Val d'Isere.

There, to-day, runs the Franco-Italian frontier, a bulwark of black rock, jagged and formidable, ironically called the ' *promenade de famille* '. The Fascist guards do not encourage stray pedestrians; in fact, it is better to stick to the French side, unless you are satisfied to cross by such recognised routes as the Grand or the little St. Bernard, or unless you are ready to risk a rifle bullet. It is no sacrifice to stick to the French side. There is room and to spare. But, evidently, one must be careful to visit it only between the feast of St. John and the feast of St. Michael, unless one is prepared to find the flowers blanketed by snow, a cow in one's bedroom, the hotel shut up, and Madame in full flight for Paris.

Note from another Country: Tuscany

O<small>NCE</small> when I made the mistake of living in London somebody wrote to me in a charmingly old-fashioned writing, with
a great many capital letters and underlinings, saying : ' What a
Torment it must be for you to live in a Town, seeing nothing but
Houses and Advertisements '. This might seem to be a simple
saying, but it sank into me and made a stain, so that I wondered
about people : how many of them, who lived in towns, really
saw nothing but houses and advertisements ? and how many of
them who led a more retired life, built up for themselves a whole
inner existence out of tiny but immensely significant occurrences ?
Montaigne, for instance, was obviously such a one, to whom even
a new thought was an event ; and in the permanent mood of an
intense inward excitement he took to his essays, as the daily
purgation of a mind which must find some outlet, so intoxicating
were the discoveries made in solitude, and came to the conclusion
that it is exceedingly difficult to say what one means. My copy
of Montaigne says on the fly-leaf : ' Mary Jones, her Husband's
Gift, 1751, price 14s. the three Volumes.' I like to reconstruct
that Mary Jones. To her, her husband, spelt with a capital letter,
was a fact ; and his gift, also spelt with a capital letter, was an
event : Her Husband presented her with the Gift of Montaigne's
Essays, nicely bound in brown leather, but on what occasion she
does not say : not an anniversary, surely, or the appended date
would have been more specific than merely 1751 : no, it must
have been an occasional gift, an unbirthday present, on a stray
day of the year ; perhaps he had been cross to her in the morning,
and, sensible of remorse, returned home in the evening with the
gift under his arm, who knows ? And the cost of the gift, he must

215

have told her that ; let it drop, as it were : fourteen shillings !
else how should she have known, as know she evidently did, for
the sum is entered in the same handwriting. Or was that writing
his, not hers ? We shall never know, nor shall we know whether
this acquisition or the perusal of that Montaigne represented an
adventure, a milestone in the life of Mary Jones ; all that we can
know is that the gift at some time, perhaps at her death, passèd
from her possession into that of Thomas Sedgwick Whalley, of
Rendip Lodge, whose bookplate adorns the end-paper ; and then
comes my name, with that of the friend who gave me the book :
a whole little palimpsest of lives, superimposed one on another
in the foxed old volume : Montaigne himself, Mary Jones,
Mr. Whalley, and then finally me.

Such speculations are possibly not worth pursuing, and the
psycho-analysts, indeed, definitely disapprove of day-dreams ; they
give them a terrible name, unco-ordinated thought or something
like that, and tell us to practise a useful concentration. But the
truth is that the adventures which happen in the mind are more
dangerous and important than those which happen outwardly in
the open air ; they have a habit of fermenting, and all sorts of
toadstools sprout in the half-light of our underground cellars.
Shall we then listen to the psycho-analysts and their warnings ?
The toadstools have their beauty. Scarlet, speckled, grotesque,
they glow in the obscure corners. It is not safe to explore underground : you do not know what you may meet.

There was an adventure which happened to me once, and
which, although it will lose everything in the telling, I will tell.
It did not take place among houses and advertisements, and those
who saw me pale with terror—those, that is, who saw the effect
without having shared the experience—laughed at me in a kindly
and comforting way. I was annoyed that they should have
found me out, for what had happened concerned me and me
only, but there was no help for it ; my looks had betrayed me.
Had I seen a ghost ? no, I had seen nothing so palpable as a ghost ;

I had in fact seen nothing at all ; I had only felt. I was careful
not to tell them this ; I simply said that I felt ill and wanted air.
So I did. But what I wanted most was time to absorb something
which I already knew I should never forget.

The place was an old Italian castle, situated down in a valley
among cypresses. The slopes of the hills, in rough terraces, were
covered with vines ; and as the month was October the leaves
had turned to a brilliant red, so that the hill-side in the level rays
of the sinking sun appeared to be on fire. It was a remote place
in the country, a deep bowl of a place, scooped in the hills ; and
that old castle, among the black trees, scarcely visible, seemed to be
trying to burrow its way even more deeply into the heart of the
earth. I am not saying that it was sinister, for it was not ; only
it was like a great piece of rock that had got lodged among the
cypresses at the bottom ; that had rolled itself down from the top
of the hills and would have liked to go deeper had the earth not
stopped it. There were no other dwellings within sight ; it was
alone with the red vines and the black cypresses and the circle of
blue sky overhead ; nor could it rightly be called a dwelling, for
the peasants used it only during the day-time and deserted it
for the night when their labour was done. It was deserted when
we came to it, but the great gate was open to a push in the thought-
less trusting way of remote country districts, and our footsteps
rang unchallenged on the stones of the inner courtyard. We
penetrated into the rooms ; they were put to purely useful
uses ; hung with grapes, that is to say, grapes that were not to be
pressed into wine, but dried into raisins, so that they were hung,
bunch after bunch, along osier wands where the maximum of
sunlight would strike upon them. Even now the afternoon sun
was on them, making them transparent as they hung, the veinings
and even the pips visible, as the veins of a hand held against the
fire. We exclaimed, and thought them lovely. But there were
deeper recesses within the castle : a flight of stone steps, leading
down, less attractive than the old banqueting rooms hung with

grapes, but more attractive because more mysterious, less obvious, more frightening. I slipped away and went down alone.

Upstairs I left the courtyard, with the late sun striking into it, and the voices of my friends ; the steps led me down into an increasing darkness, so that I reached out my hand to touch the wall lest I should stumble. I could just see that the bottom of the steps opened out into a cellar. There was a gleam of light from a cobwebbed window opposite. A dim aroma came up to me, but I thought nothing of it, and trod light-heartedly down into the cellar, and stood there among the enormous barrels, like vats, ranged on either side of the vault. I stood there, pleased to be alone in that queer place, looking at the vats, and snuffing the curiously scented air. I did not at first understand how insidious the scent was ; at first, it was sweet and heavy, neither pleasant nor unpleasant, but just different from anything I had ever smelt before. I snuffed it, interested, as one might play with a new idea. I was down there, I suppose, for two minutes before I was overcome. I had not realised that the barrels were full to the brim with fermenting juice. Even as I was seized with panic—panic in the classical sense of the word, panic in the sense of a spirit sprung from nature and stronger than myself—I did not realise it. I knew only that I must reach the air or I should fall. Blindly I turned and staggered for the steps, gasping for air, gasping above all for sanity, struggling to escape the cellar where such irresistible forces had nearly taken possession of me. I reached the top, and the hands of my friends pulled me into the light.

But what I still want to know, is, what happened to Mary Jones and Mr. Whalley when they went down into the darker places ?

THE END